READER'S DIGEST

LIFE AT THE LIMITS

D

… survives temperatures that plummet … erful bird has thick, white plumage and … it is perfectly adapted to life in the … s main food is lemmings, with the … g at least two a day during their … son. The family might get … as many as 1500 lemmings … the youngsters have … vn the nest.

HIGH AND COLD

Watermelon snow appears in summer on mountains and in the Antarctic. It has the slight smell of a fresh watermelon and a pink colour, which is caused by carotenoid pigments in the green algae that live in ice.

The chinchilla lives in the high Andes at altitudes up to 5000 m. The rabbit-sized rodent is kept warm by its dense fur coat, considered to be the finest pelage in the natural world.

-25°C

0°C

In Australia, studies of 115-million-year-old tracks of a meat-eating dinosaur indicate that some dinosaurs were possibly adapted to life in the cold. At the time the fossil footprints were made, the temperature in the area ranged from 20°C in summer to –30°C in winter, so the dinosaur might have had body fat to keep warm, just as modern mammals have today.

FASCINATING FACT

… ckest and … A generally … t muzzle, ears … s a relatively … heat can … ange system in … tain heat.

DEEP AND COLD

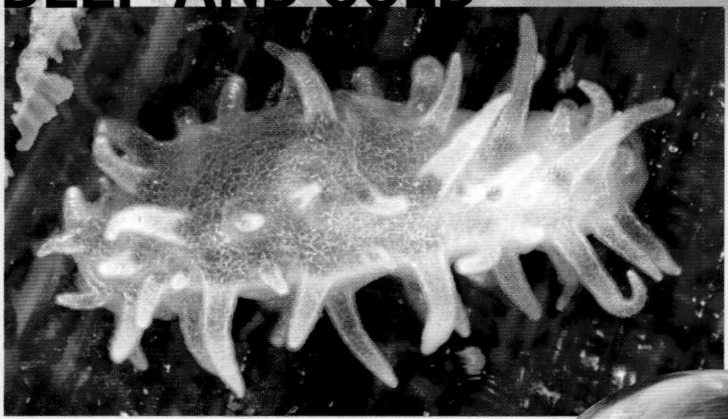

Sea cucumbers are among the few organisms living in the world's deepest oceanic trench, the Challenger Deep. The pressure at 10 923 m below the surface is 500 times that at the surface; the temperature is 2.3°C.

Polychaete worms live on a solid piece of orange methane ice at 540 m deep in the Gulf of Mexico. The ice forms on the sea floor in conditions of low temperature and high pressure.

…ntarctic dry valleys are among the driest and … dest places on Earth. Temperatures drop to –25°C and … ere is little water. It is one of the harshest habitats on … rth, yet algae, bacteria and fungi live here, not on the … rface, but inside the rocks (left). Organisms survive … ere sandwiched between wafer-thin layers just beneath the rock's surface. The spaces are like miniscule greenhouses. The habitat is so hostile, these organisms grow only on a couple of days each year.

LIFE IN EXTREMES

ICE CO

The snowy
to –62.5°C. T
feathered
Arctic. T
adults
nes
th

Some plants and animals live in the most extreme conditions. They have special adaptations that enable them to survive where other living things would simply perish. Studies of the organisms living at the very boundaries of endurance help to further our knowledge of how our planet came into being and shed vital light on the ability of life to survive on Earth in the future. There have also been useful technological spin-offs. Enzymes that function either at very high or very low temperatures are incorporated into 'biological' washing powders.

-90°C

-60°C

EXTREME COLD

Male emperor penguins incubate their eggs through the dark Antarctic winter, huddling together for warmth. Each bird has an egg balanced on its feet, and they slowly shuffle round so that each one takes a turn on the outside edge of the huddle, where it is coldest. The lowest temperature on Earth was recorded as –89.4°C at nearby Vostok base (above) on July 21, 1983. In 1997 unconfirmed reports indicated an even lower temperature of –91°C.

The arctic fox has
warmest fur of any m
rounded body shape a
and legs mean that th
small surface area fro
escape. Body fat and a he
the blood vessels of its paws h

DRY COLD

COLD

LIFE HAS FOUND A
MOST INHOSPITABLE
EXTREMES OF HOT AND
ACID, ALKALI AND SALT.
HIGHEST ALTITUDES
OCEAN DEPTHS. THE
ADAPTED TO SUCH
AT THE VERY LIMITS

FOOTHOLD IN EARTH'S
REGIONS, SURVIVING
COLD, WET AND DRY,
THERE IS LIFE AT THE
AND IN THE DARKEST
PLANTS AND ANIMALS
EXTREMES ARE LIVING
OF WHAT IS POSSIBLE.

:an deserts runs at
vn just about anything
The bird strikes so
d or dragonfly from
desert heat include an
vater from its faeces
on.

The rocks in the deserts of North America are coloured orange, green, yellow and black, so-called 'desert varnish'. The colour is from minerals deposited by colonies of bacteria that live on the bare rock. They take 10 000 years to create a thin layer of red iron oxide or black manganese oxide.

HOT

EXTREME HEAT

The bacterium Strain 121 is so-called because it thrives in hydrothermal vent water in the Pacific at a temperature of 121°C. Another bacterium survives in sediments in the deep sea at temperatures of 169°C – the highest known temperature at which life exists. The world's toughest bacterium is *Deinococcus* (below), which survives intense radioactivity.

120°C

With its surface 420 m below sea level, the Dead Sea in the Middle East is the lowest point on Earth. It is considered 'dead' because no large creatures can survive in its waters. But there are micro-organisms, such as *Halobacterium*, that live only in the very salty conditions found in enclosed bodies of water with a high salt content, such as the Dead Sea and Great Salt Lake in North America.

FASCINATING FACT

SURVIVAL SUPERSTAR

Tardigrades or water bears are superorganisms. They have survived for a few minutes in laboratory conditions at –272°C, just one degree above absolute zero, the coldest temperature that it is possible to achieve. At the other end of the scale, they have survived being heated to 151°C. This wide-ranging tolerance means that tardigrades – the biggest of which are 1.5 mm long – can live just about anywhere on Earth.

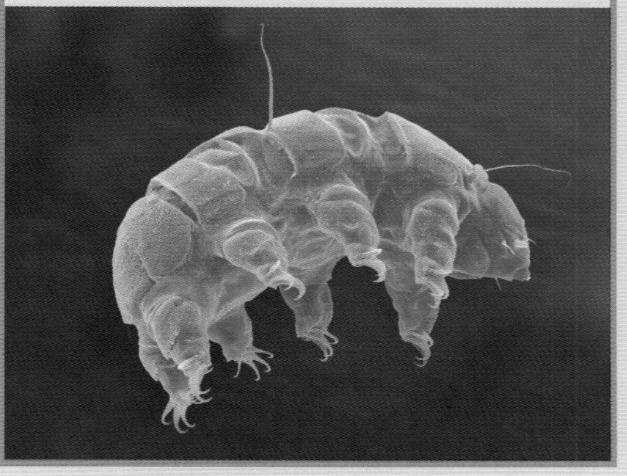

EAT

Flamingos arrive in their millions to feed and nest on the caustic surface of Lake Natron and other East African soda lakes. The birds are largely safe here from predators, because the shallow lakes are so alkaline the water burns the skin of other creatures, while the flamingos appear to be immune.

HIGH AND HOT

El Tatio in the high Andes is the highest geyser field in the world at 4300 m above sea level. Run-off from the geysers is stained red and green with bacteria. Living just a few metres from the scalding water is a dark-coloured frog with a sinister habit – it eats its neighbours.

DESERT HEA

The roadrunner of North A
speeds of up to 27 km/h and chase
it can tackle, even deadly rattlesna
fast that it can snatch a hummi
mid-air. Adaptations to
ability to reabs
before ex

25°C

50°C

The sand cat lives in the hottest and driest deserts of Africa and Asia, where the temperature can fluctuate between –5°C and 52°C. The sand cat gets all the water i needs from the rodents and lizards that it eats, while lon hair on its paws protects it from the scorching hot sand.

DEEP HEAT

The vent crab is top predator in a community that lives close to hot springs on the sea floor at depths of 2.7 km. Bacteria turn chemicals in the vent into organic materials. The crab tolerates water at a comfortable 25°C near the vents to a chilly 2°C in the surrounding seawater. It lives under high pressure and cannot survive if brought to the surface.

ALKALINE

LIFE AT THE LIMITS

1 SURVIVING HEAT

2 BELOW ZERO

5 MOUNTAIN REFUGE

6 HIGH FLIERS

3 WETLAND WORLDS

4 LIVING IN THE DARK

7 AVOIDING EXTREMES

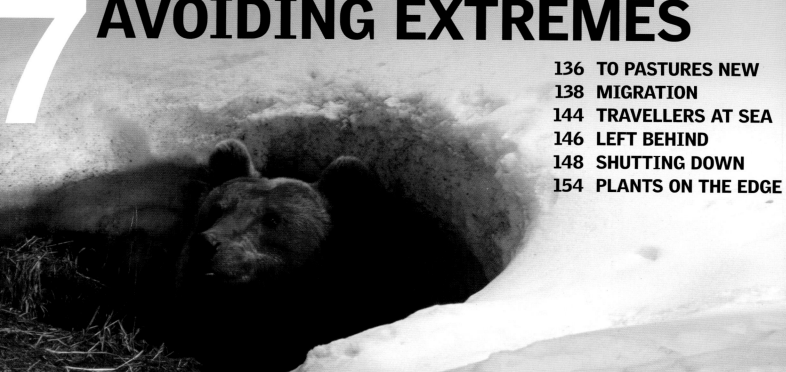

INTRODUCTION

LIFE IS EVERYWHERE ON OUR PLANET, EVEN IN PLACES WHERE IT WOULD NOT BE EXPECTED TO SURVIVE AT ALL. In every seemingly inhospitable corner there are resilient life forms that have adapted to survive extreme conditions – from unrelenting drought to piercing subzero temperatures. Some plants and animals have overcome the challenges of life at high altitudes, while others cope with persistent inundation or a salt-saturated environment.

There are birds on migration, such as cranes and geese, that fly higher than the world's highest mountains, while silken threads enable ballooning spiders to cover epic distances at **great heights**. Marine creatures, such as sea cucumbers, live under **immense pressure** in the deepest part of the ocean. Other abyssal creatures have the power to create their own light – **bioluminescent light** – which helps them to catch prey or avoid being caught in the pitch-black waters. Desert ants withstand drought, desiccation and daytime temperatures peaking at 55°C. And in the **frozen wastes** of Antarctica there is a lichen that is able to photosynthesise in temperatures as low as –12°C. The whio of New Zealand is one of a number of birds that make their home in **turbulent white waters**, while the river sharks living along the coasts of southern

Asia are saltwater–freshwater specialists. Blind cave creatures live a life in **complete darkness**, and animals living close to hot springs at the bottom of the sea depend on energy not from the Sun but from deep down in the Earth.

There are fungi in garden compost heaps that experience temperatures of 80°C, and lichens that grow on **bare rock**. Some organisms can function **without oxygen**, and others thrive on **toxic substances** that would kill most living things. There are parasites living on or inside other creatures, and 'helpful bacteria' found in stomach acids. Some **microorganisms** can live in water that is scalding or frozen, extremely acid or alkaline, salt or freshwater. Microbes have even been found in the world's deepest gold mines in South Africa, 2.8 km below the surface: they use hydrogen split from water molecules by the **radioactivity** in the deep rock. And in 1994 scientists discovered organisms living in marine sediments at temperatures of 169°C, setting a new high temperature record at which life is known to exist.

To live in such extremes, the **building blocks** of life and the **chemistry** that makes them tick must be tolerant of a broad range of conditions. For this reason, it is not unreasonable to speculate that life may not be confined to our tiny planet. We may not be alone in the universe after all.

SURVIV
HEAT

ING 1

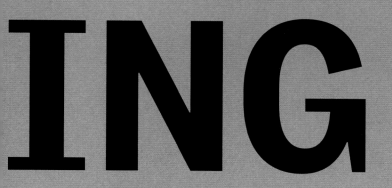

TWO GEMSBOK SEARCH FOR GRAZING IN SOUTHERN AFRICA'S NAMIB DESERT, where daytime summer temperatures soar to 40°C. Most animals need warmth to function. Reptiles and other 'cold-blooded' creatures depend on heat directly from the Sun, while the 'warm-blooded' mammals and birds generate their own heat. Warm-blooded animals can maintain a constant body temperature whether the air temperature is high or low, but they pay a price for this ability: if their body temperature rises by more than a few degrees for too long, they are in danger of overheating. Even cold-blooded animals cannot function if the temperature is too high. Apart from some 'extremophiles' that thrive in extreme conditions, animals cannot take too much heat, so those living in hot environments, like the gemsbok, have adaptations and strategies that help them to survive.

MERCURY RISING

Like all creatures in hot deserts, the gemsbok faces three problems – the danger of overheating by day, a scarcity of water and a lack of food.

WHEN THE TEMPERATURE RISES, MOST ANIMALS LEG IT FOR THE SHADE, BUT IN THE DESERT THERE IS LITTLE SHADE FOR THEM TO FIND. Many creatures living there are small – rodents, lizards, insects and spiders – and they lie buried under the sand during the heat of the day, emerging only at night, when the temperature drops. For larger animals, such as the gemsbok of southern Africa, this luxury is not available.

The gemsbok is a desert antelope, which lives exposed to the Sun's full glare. Like all creatures in hot deserts, it faces three problems – the danger of overheating by day, a scarcity of water and a lack of food. In other parts of the world, many animals, including humans, bring their body temperature down by sweating, but desert animals cannot afford to lose the water. Instead, the gemsbok is able to let its body temperature rise from a normal 35.7°C to 45°C – a level that most mammals could not survive – to delay cooling by evaporation. For food, it eats whatever vegetation is available – it can even dig up bulbs and tubers from as much as a metre under the ground. By supplementing this diet with water-rich plants, such as tsama melons and wild cucumbers, it acquires most of its water, as well as its nutrients, from the food it eats.

For flying birds, water conservation is less critical than for animals such as the gemsbok, because they can fly to reach any available open water. In hot arid regions of Africa, the Middle East and Asia, this allows the spotted sandgrouse to cope with the intense heat. A female sandgrouse incubating eggs on the open ground can be exposed to temperatures of over 50°C, yet she does not pant or gape as heat-stressed birds often do. Instead, water evaporates from her skin to keep herself and her eggs cool. The sandgrouse has also evolved an unusual way to take water to its flightless chicks. The parents, especially male birds, visit the nearest water supply, usually at dawn or dusk, and there they soak their belly feathers, which are structurally adapted to absorb and hold water. Back at the nest, the youngsters strip the water from their feathers.

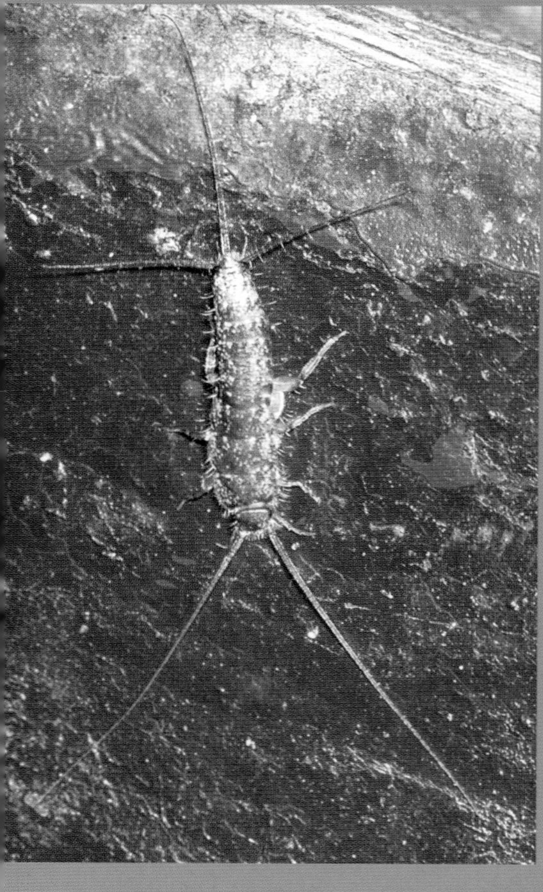

HEAT-LOVING INSECT
The firebrat (left) is at home in hot and humid conditions. It is a fast breeder and can become a serious household pest.

Heat-seekers

Some organisms, especially the infinitesimally small, positively thrive in temperatures that would kill almost any other other living thing. These are the extremophiles, lovers of extreme conditions, mainly bacteria and algae that live at the very edge of what is possible. The heat-lovers among them are 'thermophiles', and one of the first to be identified was *Pyrococcus furiosus*, meaning the 'rushing fireberry'. It was discovered in 1981 in volcanically heated sediments on a beach at Porto Levante on the small volcanic island of Vulcano, north-east of Sicily. Subsequent investigation showed that its optimum living temperature is 100°C, the temperature of boiling water – from which it gets its 'fireberry' name. The 'rushing' part of its name comes from the ability to double its number of cells in just 37 minutes.

Heat-lovers can also be found in the home. The firebrat is a small primitive, wingless insect, related to the silverfish that people sometimes find in their bathrooms. The firebrat likes heat and plenty of it, so it prefers the kitchen. It lives close to heating pipes, fireplaces, domestic boilers, bakers' ovens and industrial furnaces. The female is particularly fussy. She will only lay her eggs when the temperature is 32–41°C. At about 1.5 cm long, the firebrat is not easy to spot. It is mainly nocturnal, prefers dark surfaces to light ones, runs rapidly and hides in small crevices. It eats mainly carbohydrates, from flour to book bindings, so its chief claim to fame is as a nuisance.

DUTIFUL MOTHER A gilded flicker spreads her wings to shade the eggs or chicks in the nest she has excavated in a saguaro cactus. The flicker is a species of woodpecker living in the deserts of the south-western USA.

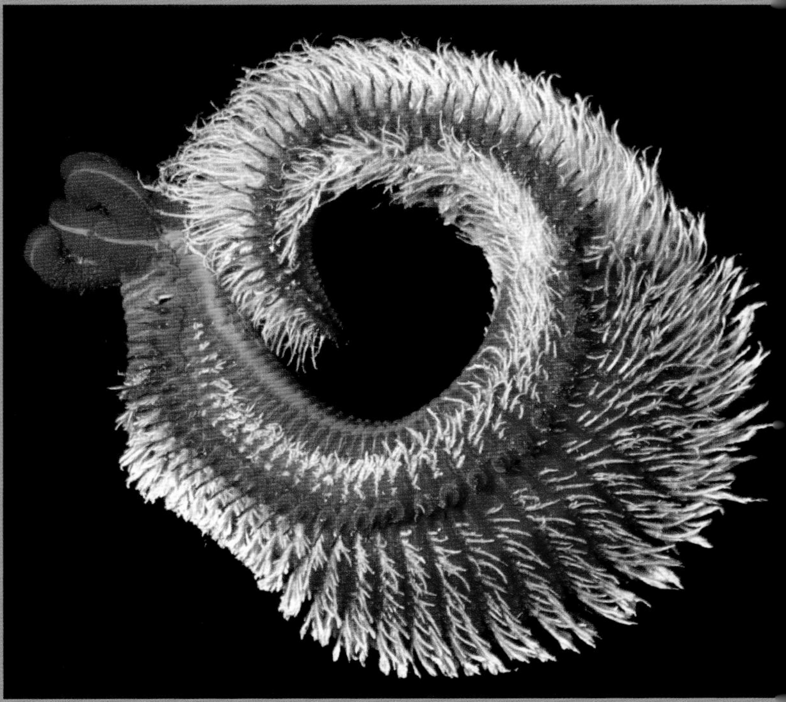

HOT TAIL The Pompeii worm lives close to hot springs on the deep-sea floor. Only 13 cm long, it manages to position itself so that its tail is in water at 80°C while its head is at just 22°C.

THERMAL TIGHTROPE

FOR THE SAHARAN SILVER ANT, EXTREME HEAT IS AN ALLY IN THE DAILY BATTLE FOR SURVIVAL, helping it to find food and minimising the risk of becoming food itself. While many desert animals restrict their foraging to the cooler periods around dawn and dusk, the silver ant opts for the opposite tactic. In the few minutes at the hottest part of the day, when the air temperature in the Sahara soars to 60°C, silver ant foragers leave their underground nests in an explosive outburst. With most of their predators, such as desert lizards, keeping out of the Sun, they have a small window of food-finding opportunity. So long as they can withstand the pressure from heat stress, which could kill them, they are safe from predators, which could also kill them.

Balancing these two risks and exploiting the opportunities they make available requires skill and special adaptations. Because the time slot is so small, the ants need to be good navigators, able to race back to their nests without hesitating once their time is up. In the flat terrain of the Sahara, there are few landmarks to help them to find their way home, and odour trails, used by many other animals, evaporate quickly in the heat. Instead, the ants have a kind of internal pedometer that enables them to keep track of how many steps they have taken – and therefore how many steps they need to take to get back to the nest. To help them to keep a track of direction, they observe the patterns of sunlight reflected from the desert's surface.

Exceptionally long legs keep the ants' tiny bodies about 0.6 cm above the burning desert floor and also help to propel them rapidly to and from the nest. The ants do not walk, but sprint everywhere, reaching speeds of a hundred times their body length per second, which makes them one of the world's fastest animals. They race in straight lines, making brief stops occasionally and performing little pirouettes to check their bearings.

Soaring, gliding and fanning

Despite these adaptations, life is not easy for the silver ants, and many individuals die. Creatures like them walk a tightrope – too little heat and they fail to operate effectively; too much and they

SAND HUNTER A desert monitor forages among Saharan dunes. Its nostrils are close to its eyes rather than on the tip of its snout. This helps it to breathe when buried in the sand during the heat of the day.

HEAT DEFENCE Japanese honeybees work together to defend their hive against an attack by an Asian giant hornet. They smother the hornet and create enough heat with their bodies to kill it.

die. By taking risks with the heat, they are at the very boundaries of what is possible. Large birds such as eagles and vultures are generally in a stronger position to survive. Yet they, too, take advantage of heat to find food, using thermals – columns of hot air rising over the Sun-baked ground – to help them to soar on their large, wide wings across the landscape. Over dry desert areas, thermals do not go straight up into the air, but form tight spirals, sometimes no more than 10 m across – mini-whirlwinds called dust devils often rush across the ground at their bases. As a result, the birds have to fly in tight circles to remain in the rising column. Then, when they reach cruising height, they leave the column and glide some distance, losing height as they go. After a while, they grab a lift in another warm air column and continue on their way. In this way, these birds can travel great distances without the effort of a single wing beat, all the while searching for prey or carrion down below – turkey vultures in North America, for example, regularly travel 30 km from their nest or roost. Soaring also enables the birds to escape the high midday temperatures closer to the ground.

In a cooler climate, another set of winged creatures uses heat as a defence against predators. In Japan, giant hornets often target the hives of honeybees. When this happens, small groups of about 500 bees gather around the invaders, each bee vibrating its flight muscles to generate heat. At the centre of the group, the temperature is raised to about 47°C, which the bees can tolerate but the hornet cannot. The hornet's threshold is 45°C – any higher and it is baked to death. On these two degrees of heat hangs the fate of the honeybee colony. If the bees fail to raise the temperature sufficiently, the hornet survives and summons its own nest mates. Each hornet kills bees at a rate of 40 a minute, so a colony is quickly exterminated and its larvae are taken as hornet food.

SHADY COMPANY *A pride of lions squeeze into a small patch of shade to escape the desert heat in the Mombo area of Botswana's Okavango Delta.*

DEGREES OF SHADE

UNDER THE HOT AFRICAN SUN, LIONS SEEK ANY SHADE THEY CAN FIND – USUALLY FROM A TREE OR ROCKY OUTCROP. For them as for countless other animals, finding shade is an essential way to escape the heat of the day and save energy. In tourist areas, lions sometimes use the shade of safari vehicles, and at bush airstrips, prides have been known to lie under aircraft wings.

Portable parasol

In the hot, arid regions of southern Africa, the Cape ground squirrel carries its own shade with it. Active by day, the squirrel is exposed to very high temperatures as it forages on the ground for small plants and seeds, so it uses its bushy tail, which is nearly as long as its body, as a parasol. The shape of the tail – combined with a certain resemblance to the unrelated meerkat – has given rise to the squirrel's common name

Beneath the Cape ground squirrel's tail, the temperature can be 5°C lower than the ambient air temperature. This gives the squirrel a key advantage in the foraging stakes, as it can be active for longer than other animals of a similar size.

THE GIBBERBIRD

Shade is in rare supply in the stony wilderness of Australia's gibber deserts, such as the Sturt Stony Desert, where a few grasses and saltbushes grow amidst closely spaced layers of wind-polished stones (or gibbers). Yet even in these harsh conditions a few animals manage to survive, including the gibberbird or gibber chat (right), a kind of honeyeater. A small yellow-breasted bird with long, delicate legs, the gibberbird avoids the deserts' few predators – such as the kowari, an endangered carnivorous marsupial – simply by tucking in its head and turning its back. Its camouflaged plumage does the rest. Other gibber desert creatures include the fat-tailed dunnart – a mouse-like marsupial, which stores fat in its carrot-shaped tail for times of food shortage – the fawn-hopping mouse and the well-camouflaged dotterel. The dotterel nests in the gibber deserts, but often does so in the middle of long, desert roads, earning it the nickname of 'suicide bird'.

in Afrikaans: *waaierstert meerkat*, 'fan-tailed meerkat'. The tail serves its sunshade purpose very effectively. If the temperature rises above 40°C, the squirrel simply turns its back on the Sun and raises its tail over its head. Beneath the tail, the temperature can be 5°C lower than the ambient air temperature. This gives the squirrel a key advantage in the foraging stakes, as it can be active for longer. While other animals of a similar size only forage for an average of three hours each day, Cape ground squirrels can keep going for seven, emerging about an hour after sunrise and retiring about 30 minutes before sunset. Even they cannot cope with the hottest part of the day and they take a break at midday, heading for their burrows at a time when the temperature even in the shade of their tails exceeds 40°C.

Ground squirrels are highly social animals and they also use their tails as part of their body language for communicating with each other. When danger threatens, a squirrel waves its tail up and down while giving an alarm whistle.

Reptile adaptations

Reptiles are mainly cold blooded, which means that they control body temperature by moving in or out of the Sun, but some, such as desert rattlesnakes, have additional abilities. Their skins are slightly darker in the morning, when they need to warm up quickly to a temperature at which they can function – darker colours absorb more heat energy than lighter ones. The skin becomes paler as the day goes on. There is still a danger that the snakes could overheat at the hottest time around midday, so they find shade to lower their body temperature. They manage to maintain a remarkably stable body temperature – much more stable than the surrounding air temperature.

SHADY TAIL A Cape ground squirrel in the Namib Desert turns its back on the Sun and spreads out its bushy tail as a shade. The sunshade also helps disguise the squirrel from eagles and hawks.

COOL OF THE NIGHT

NIGHT-TIME IS WHEN THE HOT DESERT COMES ALIVE. Plant-eaters emerge from their tunnels and burrows to forage in the relative coolness, and meat-eaters come out to hunt them. In the deserts of south-western North America, one of the nocturnal vegetarians is the black-tailed jackrabbit – in fact, a kind of hare. Having spent most of the day resting in a shallow scrape, or 'form', at the base of a shrub or bush, the jackrabbit is up and about at dusk and carries on foraging well into the night. While doing so, it is always on the alert, preferring open spaces where it can spot night-time predators, such as coyotes and hawks, while they are still some distance away. With a top speed of about 58 km/h, the jackrabbit can outrun and out-manoeuvre most pursuers. It has fur on the soles of its feet, which allows it to run even on hot sand. The jackrabbit's enormous ears are another adaptation for the heat – by increasing or decreasing the blood flow to the ears, it can regulate its body temperature. It conserves water by eating its food twice – first, the vegetation itself, then its own

DESERT FOX The African bat-eared fox has large ears to locate insects and small teeth with which to chew them. In summer, it shelters from the daytime heat in a burrow, coming out at night to forage.

SAND LEAPER The desert jerboa is a small rodent with large hind legs and furry feet that act like snowshoes on sand. Living in Africa and western Asia, it is active at night, searching for seeds and other plant material.

droppings. The jackrabbit rarely drinks, obtaining most of its water from the plants it eats, such as cactus and sagebrush.

Night fliers

When darkness falls over the Sonoran Desert straddling the US–Mexican border two species of nightjar, the lesser nighthawk and common poorwill, come out to hunt. The nighthawk flies silently and low, searching for flying insects like a bat, while the poorwill conserves its energies. For most of the time, it sits on the ground, watching for the silhouettes of moths and beetles. When it spots a target, it flies up and grabs the victim in its mouth. Both birds have large eyes and need some light to hunt by – the poorwill, in particular, prefers moonlit nights. In the winter, when the temperature in the desert plunges, the nighthawk migrates to warmer regions, but the poorwill stays behind. It is the only bird known to hibernate – in hollows in desert rocks.

The Sonoran Desert is also home to large nocturnal centipedes, up to 20 cm long. The giant desert centipede is black with an orange head and tail. Its last pair of legs is also orange and resembles antennae, making it difficult for a predator to work out which end is the head and which the tail. Its own prey includes insects, lizards and even small rodents. It catches them by running them down, then kills by injecting venom using large pincer-like 'fangs' – actually modified front legs.

Plants, too, come to life at night. The queen of the night or night-blooming cereus is a cactus that looks dead most of the time. But at dusk on one midsummer night a year, it produces exquisitely scented, white, trumpet-shaped flowers. The flowers attract night-flying moths, which help to pollinate the plant. By dawn, the flowers have closed and will not reappear for another year.

Big ears

In the hot plains and deserts of eastern and southern Africa, two populations of a small species of fox are mainly active at night. Bat-eared foxes – so called because of their large, wide ears – are unusual among foxes in that they have mostly forsaken mammalian prey in favour of insects, chiefly termites and grasshoppers. Their large ears serve two purposes – they help to keep them cool and they also give the foxes a keen sense of hearing, which they use to locate their insect prey. The foxes are attracted by swarming locusts and they also stake out large plains herbivores, such as zebras and antelopes – not to feast on the animals, but to catch the insects attracted to their dung.

Another creature whose ears are thought to dissipate body heat is the long-eared hedgehog. One of several species of desert hedgehog, it lives in deserts and arid grasslands in the Middle East, parts of India and Central Asia. By day, it hides in burrows and rocky cliffs, but at night it will wander for 9 km or more in search of food, including invertebrates, eggs and fruit. Desert hedgehogs are active when conditions are right for foraging, but should the temperature either soar or plummet, they go into a state of torpor until things pick up again.

SPIKY FORAGER Several hedgehog species have adapted to desert conditions. Native to northern Africa and western Asia, Paraechinus aethiopicus *is the smallest, just 15–28 cm long,*

COOLING SYSTEMS

DESERT NOMADS Namib elephants undertake five-day treks across the desert between the Skeleton Coast, where they feast on the pods of the ana tree, and the Kabere Mountains, where myrrh bushes are a treat.

MUD BATHING A liberal coating of mud keeps a baby elephant cool. It is also good for its skin and stops insects from biting. If mud is available, elephants will bathe in it several times a day.

WHILE MOST ANIMALS TRY TO STAY OUT OF THE HEAT, THE LARGEST HAVE AN OBVIOUS DIFFICULTY IN HIDING FROM THE SUN – they are just too big and some of the places where they live have little shade.

In the Namib Desert in south-western Africa, this is a problem that faces the world's largest land-dwelling animal – the elephant. At 55 million years old, the Namib is the oldest desert on the planet. It is a landscape of shifting sand dunes, gravel plains and rugged mountains. It has a sparse and unpredictable pattern of rainfall, with prolonged periods of drought; rivers can appear briefly above ground and then disappear below again just as suddenly.

A variety of adaptations enable the elephants of the Namib to survive these conditions, the harshest endured by any elephant population. One is their ears. African bush elephants, the species that live in the Namib, have enormous ears, three times as large as those of their Asian relatives. Criss-crossed by networks of small blood vessels that bring hot blood close to the surface, they work on the same principle as a car radiator. Heat from the blood is lost to the outside through the thin layer of skin on the back of each ear. The cooler blood from the ears then rejoins the general circulation. The elephant also flaps its ears to help the air to flow over them. In addition to this, elephants spray themselves with water – as the water evaporates, it cools the body. If water is not available in the surrounding terrain, they spray themselves from water pouches hidden in their throats, which act as a kind of reserve supply.

Penguin problems

For penguins, the danger of overheating comes from their adaptation to a life in water, rather than on the land. Although some penguin species live in the Antarctic, several are found in warmer climes, but wherever they live, even in the Antarctic, penguins have same problem – how can such well-insulated creatures keep cool when they leave the water to nest and moult? On land, they walk around in what amounts to a feather wetsuit, which means that they could easily overheat. In Chile and Peru, Humboldt penguins excavate burrows, where they can both lay their eggs and keep out of the Sun. Galápagos penguins, which live almost on the Equator, nest in cracks in solidified lava. Yellow-eyed penguins on New Zealand's South Island nest in forests – they like low-lying vegetation at most about a metre above the ground, which gives the best shade.

Other cooling techniques include panting. Like other birds, some penguin species, such as the Adélie of the Antarctic, pant on cue, starting at the same time every day, usually just after noon. Another technique involves the positioning of their feet and flippers. In New Zealand, when yellow-eyed penguins want to lose heat, they hold their flippers out at an angle of 45 degrees. The undersides of the flippers and feet turn pink as blood vessels in them dilate and heat is lost. Yellow-eyed penguin chicks seek out marshland and stand with their feet in water.

FACTS

A HOUSE SPARROW PANTS AT 57 BREATHS PER MINUTE when air temperature stands at 30°C. The rate increases to 160 breaths a minute if the temperature goes up to 43°C. Some birds can pant at 1000 breaths per minute.

FUR COATS can act as insulation, helping large desert mammals to stay cool. The temperature in a camel's outermost layer of hair may be 30°C higher than its body temperature.

IN HUMANS, normal body temperature is 36–37°C. Death is certain if body temperature rises to 45°C. An average adult human loses 1–1.5 litres of water an hour when sweating.

FACTS

Seals and sea lions have a similar problem. They have thick layers of blubber under the skin and a thick pelt to insulate them from prolonged exposure to cold water – the largest seal, the elephant seal, has 15 cm of blubber beneath its waterproof fur coat. As a result, when they haul themselves out of the surf to breed or moult, they are in real danger of overheating, especially as shade is scarce on beaches. The elephant seal remains inactive for long periods of the day, occasionally using its flippers to sweep damp sand or gravel over its body. This not only helps to cool down the seal's huge body, but also provides a sunscreen to protect the skin.

Large bull elephant seals competing for mates wallow in tide pools to cool down after fighting. The bulls that have lost their fights tend to go to a 'losers' beach', where they hang about waiting for a chance to fight again, covering themselves with sand or wallowing in the surf to keep cool. Recently weaned pups wallow in the shallows, too. Females give birth, rear their pups, then mate and return to the sea as quickly as possible, minimising the time they have to endure the heat – about five weeks.

Cool diggings

Land mammals have a variety of tricks to keep cool. The Arabian oryx is an antelope that lives in the deserts of the Arabian Peninsula. One of the few trees that grows in this region is the evergreen *Maerua crassifolia*, and whenever possible, the oryx rests in its shade. If no trees are available, the oryx digs down to the cooler sand below the surface and sits in the depression it has created. In and around the Sahara, its distant relative, the Dorcas gazelle, has long, slender legs and unusually long ears, adaptations that maximise cooling in the breeze. It avoids the heat of the day by foraging mainly at night.

SAND BATHING Seals flip sand over themselves to prevent the Sun from burning them and to keep cool. Sometimes, they wave their flippers in the air, letting heat escape from blood vessels in the flippers.

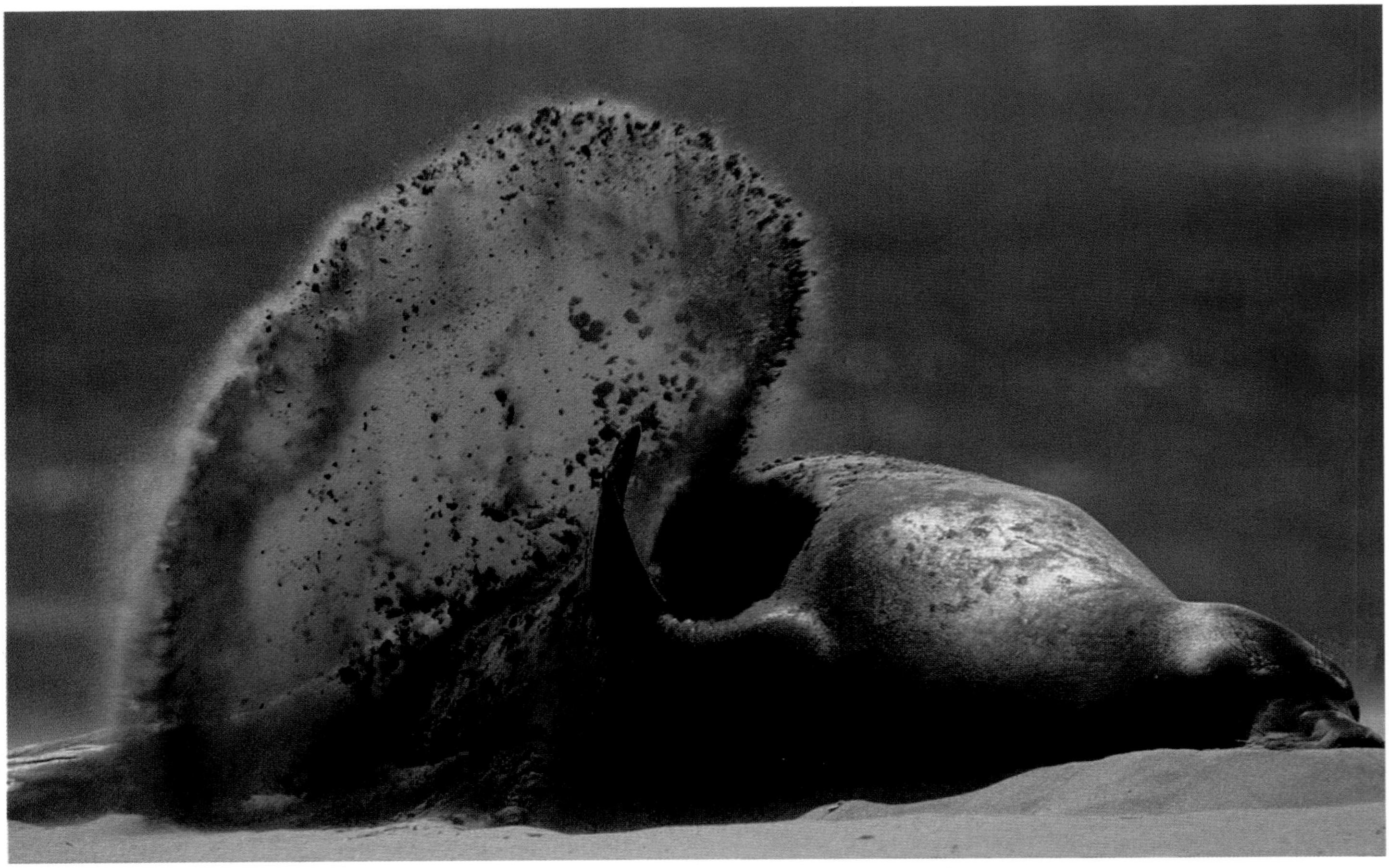

BACTRIAN CAMEL

THE ULTIMATE DESERT ANIMAL IS THE CAMEL. MOST CAMELS ARE DOMESTICATED, BUT A FEW HERDS OF WILD TWO-HUMPED BACTRIAN CAMELS SURVIVE IN THE GOBI DESERT of southern Mongolia and northern China and on dry steppe grasslands in north-western China. These camels have to cope with extremes of both heat and cold. In summer, the temperature can be over 50°C; in winter, it plunges to –30°C. This means that they need a long-haired coat in winter, which they then shed (like the camel on the right, below) at the beginning of summer for a thinner, hot-weather coat.

During the summer months, a camel's body temperature can swing between 34°C and 41°C during the day. If it needs to sweat to bring down its body temperature, it can afford to lose 25 per cent of the water in its body – a colossal amount compared with most other mammals, which dehydrate if they lose just 3–4 per cent. Yet the camel's blood remains hydrated, even though the rest of its body is losing water. When water is available, a camel can drink huge quantities very quickly – 135 litres in 15 minutes. It then retains the liquid in its kidneys and intestine – the humps store fats, not water. After taking on that amount of water, a camel can go for up to 10 days without it. To reduce water loss, its urine is like syrup while its droppings are dry enough to fuel campfires. The nostrils heat incoming air and cool outgoing air, which also reduces water loss.

VITAL STATISTICS

CLASS: Mammalia
ORDER: Artiodactyla
SPECIES: *Camelus bactrianus*
HABITAT: Cold desert and dry steppe
DISTRIBUTION: Mongolia and China
KEY FEATURE: Two humps and a long, thick winter coat. It is endangered, with fewer than 1000 individuals surviving in the wild.

Other mammals sweat or pant to keep cool. Humans, apes, monkeys and some others have sweat glands under the skin that secrete salty water. When this spreads on the surface of the skin, the evaporation causes the temperature of the skin to drop. At the same time, the hairs on the skin lie flat, preventing heat from being trapped in the still air next to the skin. The flattened hairs also help to increase the flow of air over the skin so that heat is lost by conduction and convection. Dogs, foxes and wolves cannot sweat, so they lose water via the tongue. The tongue lolls out of the mouth as the animal pants to push air across it. Many rodents, such as ground squirrels, go 'belly-basking'. They find a cool spot on the ground and flatten their bodies against it to cool down. Baboons in the Namib do the same.

In the Australian Outback, the red kangaroo can pant and sweat and has another way of keeping cool. Blood is redirected to its forelimbs, where blood vessels come close to the surface, and it licks the fur there to increase heat loss by evaporation. On very hot days, a red kangaroo stands with its body crouched and tail pulled under to minimise the surface area exposed to the Sun.

Bird measures

Africa's ostrich, the world's largest bird, lives and forages on open grassland, fully exposed to the Sun. So when temperatures soar, it needs an array of techniques and adaptations to stay cool. These include a long naked neck and long scaly legs with featherless thighs, which help it to lose heat, especially if there is a breeze. The long feathers on its back stand up when the skin is warm, creating an insulating layer between incoming solar radiation and the skin. At the same time, the gaps between the feathers allow more air movement across the skin. Other ostrich cooling tricks are to stand with its back facing away from the Sun and to droop its wings forwards and downwards to shield its chest and thighs and maximise heat loss from them.

Smaller birds have a range of options. Many pant, breathing quickly to allow cool air to pass through their lungs and air sacs while inhaling, and hot air to be expelled while exhaling. A bird with its bill open on a hot day is probably panting – it may increase its breathing rate by up to ten times. Many birds 'flutter' their throats – behaviour known as 'gular fluttering' – by flexing the hyoid bone in the neck. Because there are plenty of blood vessels in the throat's mucous membranes, a bird can lose heat in this way. In chickens, fluttering accounts for about 35 per cent of heat loss.

Birds also fluff up their feathers and hold out their wings. This enables the air to flow more freely between the feathers and skin. Some, such as albatrosses, cool their legs by shading them with their wings. Herring gulls orientate their bodies so that their white backs reflect the Sun. Egyptian plovers wet their feathers to cool themselves and their eggs or chicks. The North American turkey vulture and some storks have another unusual way of keeping cool – by defecating on the scaly part of their legs. The evaporating water cools the blood in vessels in the legs and this is circulated back into the body.

Breezing and fanning

Most reptiles lose heat by heading for the shade, but a few have behavioural adaptations that help them to cool down. The Namib day gecko has developed a specialised behaviour called 'breezing'. If a breeze blows during the hottest part of the day, the gecko stands on the highest part of a rock and lifts its body as high as possible above the surface. Heat is lost by convection in the wind.

Among insects, worker honeybees station themselves at the entrance to a hive and fan their wings to drive air through it and cool it down. Water in the pollen and nectar that they bring back to the hive evaporates to help the cooling process,

DRIBBLE AND COOL *The African shoebill stork uses its large beak to carry water back to its nest, where it dribbles the water over its eggs or chicks to help to keep them cool.*

ARM LICKING COOL A red kangaroo licks its forearm to help it cool down in the intense heat of the Outback in western New South Wales.

COOL BIRD The ostrich's naked legs help it to keep cool and it also achieves the remarkable feat of exhaling unsaturated air, conserving about 25 per cent of its daily intake of water.

and any gaps in the hive are blocked with a waxy material, called propolis, to maintain the correct airflow. Termites go one better and have in-built air-conditioning in their mounds. As hot air in the mound is lost through the mound walls, cooler air is drawn in from the bottom to replace it.

In the Namib Desert, the beetle *Stenocara* loses heat by standing in the breeze on long stilt-like legs. It regulates its temperature by placing its body close to the sand to warm up and away from the sand to cool down. When its legs are extended, the air blowing through them helps it to lose heat. Another beetle, *Onymacris*, forces air over its body by running very fast. It is one of the fastest-running insects on land.

In North America, the Sonoran Desert cicada is an oddity amongst insects. It 'sweats' through specialised pores in its cuticle. The system works as long as the cicada can suck plant sap to replace the water it is losing. This enables it to be active in the hottest part of the day.

USING WATER WISELY

STOUT LIZARD The Gila monster stores water in its fat tail as well as its body. Growing up to about 60 cm long, the reptile can swallow small birds and other, smaller lizards whole.

IF YOU PUT A WET SPONGE OUT IN THE SUN, IT WILL SOON TURN CRISP AND DRY. Desert inhabitants, from invertebrates to reptiles to mammals, contain a similar proportion of water, yet they can withstand the same conditions without drying out. Some of the smaller invertebrates, in particular, are beautifully adapted to conserve water. Insects, scorpions, spiders and their relatives have external skeletons made of chitin, a derivative of glucose, which keep the water in and the heat out.

Water is essential for all animals to function, wherever they are. In the desert, water is also vital to help animals to keep cool. The Gila (pronounced 'HEE-la') monster is a venomous, ground-dwelling lizard that lives in the Sonoran Desert of Arizona and Mexico, feeding on snakes, smaller lizards and small mammals and birds. In summer, it becomes active at dusk, but temperatures at sundown in the desert can still be as high as 40°C, and they remain above 35°C for several hours into the night. So the Gila monster needs to cool itself down even at these times. It does this by causing water to evaporate from its cloaca, the vent on its underside. The Gila monster is also able to store water. When it rains, it becomes a binge drinker, imbibing about 15–20 per cent of its body mass in a few minutes. It stores the water as dilute urine in its bladder, which becomes, in effect, a reservoir, contributing up to 20 per cent of the lizard's body weight. During a drought of 80 days or more, it can absorb that water into its blood system to stave off the effects of dehydration – Gila monsters with full bladders dehydrate 2.5 times slower than ones with empty bladders.

Another desert reptile, the Texas desert tortoise, is a herbivore, which obtains most of its water from the grasses and

REFUELLING STOP Brown-veined white butterflies migrate across large distances in Africa and southern Asia. Here, a group drink from a patch of damp ground while migrating across a southern African desert.

other desert plants it feeds on. Like the Gila monster, it has a large bladder, which stores about 40 per cent of the tortoise's body weight as dilute urine. Its scales and carapace (shell) help to stop the moisture from escaping. During the hottest and driest times of the year, the tortoise sits dormant in its burrow, where the humidity tends to be high so it loses little water.

Digging deep

Even though amphibians need water to reproduce – somewhere for their tadpoles to develop – some manage to exist in the desert, generally in places where water accumulates at certain times of the year. During the rest of the year, they lie in a kind of suspended animation buried under the desert floor. In Australia, the water-holding frog digs into the ground, where it lines its burrow and surrounds itself with mucous envelopes to retain moisture. North America's spadefoot toad digs down as much as a metre to find moist conditions and can be underground for nine months before rain finally falls. While buried, these frogs and toads produce urea, a salt-rich compound also found in mammal urine. This draws water into their bodies from the surrounding soil by osmosis – the process by which water passes from a region low in salts to one high in salts. They also store water as dilute urine in the bladder.

In deserts, small mammals spend the greater part of the day hiding in burrows or rock crevices, partly because the temperature is lower than outside, partly because the animals' breath raises the humidity inside these shelters. If, despite these precautions, a mouse or rat-sized mammal is caught out in the open and the temperature is rising, it cannot afford to lose water by sweating. With its small body size and large surface area, it would lose water so fast that it might die. Instead, some of these animals have other emergency measures to call upon. The kangaroo rat, for example, produces saliva with which it wets the fur on its chin and throat. The animal cools as the water evaporates and its exhaled breath is cooled as it passes through the throat, so that little water is lost when breathing. It also avoids moisture loss by producing very concentrated urine and dry droppings.

The kangaroo rat can survive on a relatively dry diet of plant seeds for its entire life. Most of the water it obtains is 'metabolic water', produced as a by-product of its own food-processing system.

SLOW PROGRESS A Texas desert tortoise leaves tracks in the sand at Laguna Madre in Mexico. It stores water in its bladder.

HEAT-BEATING PLANTS

DIFFERENT PLANTS HAVE DIFFERENT STRATEGIES FOR SURVIVING IN HOT, DRY CONDITIONS. Some, notably the cacti, store water when it becomes available, then live off their in-built reservoirs until the next downpour. Vertical woody ribs in the centre of a cactus keep the plant upright, and surrounding these is the water-holding tissue, encased in a thick, waxy skin that prevents moisture loss. When rains come, the cactus rapidly grows new roots, sometimes within just two hours of the downpour. The salt concentration in the root system is high, so water is absorbed immediately by osmosis and in the greatest quantity. A large cactus – such as the tree-sized saguaro in the deserts of south-western North America – can absorb as much as 3000 litres of water in the ten days after a storm, enough to keep it going for over a year without rain.

In most plants, the photosynthetic cells responsible for turning energy from sunlight into chemical energy are in the leaves, but cacti have them in the stem. Cacti leaves are sharp spines, reducing the plant's surface area and so preventing water loss. Many cacti, such as the dry whisky or dumpling cactus, have spherical rather than elongated stems to combine the highest volume with the lowest surface area. Another adaptation is the way that cacti undergo transpiration – the evaporation of water. Cacti do not transpire during the day, as most other plants do. Their stomata – the tiny pores through which they transpire – open at night, when the air is relatively cool and humid, which again reduces water loss.

Long life and resurrection

The *Welwitschia* plant, which grows in the deserts of southern Angola and western Namibia, picks up moisture from the coastal fogs that drift in from the Atlantic Ocean. The plant consists of a stem and root resembling a large woody parsnip, with just the

BACK TO LIFE The clubmoss Selaginella lepidophylla *lives in the deserts of south-western North America. In dry conditions, it stops growing and curls into a brownish ball of dried leaves (below, left). When rain comes, the leaves spread out into green, frond-like rosettes and growth continues (below, right).*

top showing. The top of the stem is concave and disc-shaped, while the root may go down as far as 30 m, seeking out any available groundwater. The plant's strangest feature is its leaves, which grow in pairs – broad, strap-shaped and continuously expanding for the entire life of the plant, adding another 13 m^2 of leaf each year. In some specimens, thought to be 1500–2000 years old, the leaves are extremely large. They also tend to be very tattered, because of damage by wind-blown sand.

The North American desert clubmoss *Selaginella lepidophylla* and the fern *Actiniopteris semiflabellata*, which lives on exposed rock faces in parts of East Africa, are plants that can withstand complete dehydration. They become dry and crisp during hot, dry conditions, and then when water becomes available, they green up and start to grow again. These species of so-called resurrection plant are often sold in nurseries and garden centres.

LEAF MOUND The battered leaves of a Welwitschia *plant sprawl across the desert sand in Namibia. The largest known* Welwitschia *is 1.4 m high.*

In the Negev and other west Asian deserts, another resurrection plant is *Anastatica hierochuntica* – also called the rose of Jericho. This dries after the rainy season and curls up its stems and seedpods into a tight, dry ball to prevent the seeds from being dispersed prematurely during the coming dry season. When the rains come again, the rainwater hits the ball and the branches spread out. At the same time, the raindrops hit spoon-like appendages on the seeds and these are splashed out, so new plants can germinate. The name 'resurrection plant' is not an entirely accurate description for *Anastatica hierochuntica*. It is actually an annual – like its relative, the cauliflower – which dies after it has set its seeds and dispersed them. The plant does not re-grow when water is added – rather the water simply straightens out the woody xylem tissues, allowing the seeds to disperse in conditions favourable for germination.

Water-storing succulents

Water-retaining plants adapted to dry climates are called succulents. Some, like cacti, store water in their stems, others in their leaves or roots. Various agave, yucca and aloe plants, for example, store water in their fleshy leaves. One of these is the century plant, or American agave, which gets its common name from the length of time it takes for its flowers to appear – not, in fact, a century, but about once every 30 years. The plant stores its water in a rosette of thick, fleshy, sword-shaped leaves, each of which is composed mainly of groups of water-storage cells. The stored sap of its relative, the blue or tequila agave, is the base ingredient for the Mexican drink tequila.

The *Yucca* genus includes the Joshua tree of south-western North America, which has a trunk made up of thousands of small fibres. The tree grows up to 15 m tall and lives for 300 years or more. Its relative, the soaptree yucca, has long, narrow, non-succulent leaves, and stores water in its main stem and roots. The plant gets its name from soap-like compounds called saponins in its trunk and roots, once used by indigenous Indians as natural shampoos and soaps.

In south-western Africa's Namib Desert, the kokerboom or quiver tree is one of the largest species of aloe, growing up to 9 m tall. It has smooth branches covered in a whitish powder that reflects sunlight away from the plant. The bark is smooth but flakes away in largish scales with very sharp edges. Water is stored in the light, spongy pith inside. Numerous branches forking off from each other create a large crown, which sometimes holds the enormous thatched nest of sociable weaver birds. It is called the quiver tree because the San (Bushmen) hollow out its tubular branches to make quivers (*kokerboom* in Afrikaans) for their arrows. A large piece of hollowed-out quiver treetrunk is said to make an effective fridge in which to store food.

NAMIB SUNSET Three quiver trees stand out against a pink dusk sky in the Namib Desert. The trees' blue-green leaves grow in rosettes at the end of forked branches. In June and July, they blossom with bright yellow flowers.

The kokerboom has an even larger relative, the bastard quiver tree, which grows up to 10 m tall. This has only a few tubular branches reaching skywards from a cone-shaped trunk – a dramatic tree on a desolate landscape. The Namib is also home to pebble plants from the genus *Lithops*, which have two bulbous leaves that store water and resemble stones. The bottle-shaped tree, *Moringa ovalifolia*, also from Namibia, has an enlarged stem for water storage and a silvery bark that reflects the Sun's rays.

In Mexico's Baja California, the boojum tree or cirio is a stem succulent – the water it stores in its stem tissues keeps it alive, dormant but healthy, in an extremely dry habitat. The boojum tree stands up to 20 m tall and resembles a long, slender, upside-down, yellow-grey carrot. The trunk has many small branches at right angles, and these are covered in tiny leaves. A similar species is the ocotillo, with wand-like stems studded with long spines arranged in a spiral.

The most unusual succulents are found on the remote and arid islands of Socotra, off the tip of the Horn of Africa. They include the dragon's blood tree, which resembles a large inside-out umbrella. The spokes are branches that channel any rainwater falling on the leaves onto the plant's roots. The stem stores water, too. The Socotra fig and desert rose have large bottle-shaped trunks that keep the plants supplied with water during the summer. There is even a cucumber tree, with squash-like fruit hanging from its branches, and a woody cabbage.

TREE FROM WONDERLAND The boojum tree owes its common name to Godfrey Sykes of Tucson's Desert Botanical Laboratory. Its fantastical shape inspired him to name it after a fictional monster in a Lewis Carroll poem, 'The Hunting of the Snark'.

BELOW ZERO

2

A MOTHER POLAR BEAR AND HER CUB CROSS AN ICEFIELD NEAR CHURCHILL IN MANITOBA, CANADA. Heat is the energy that keeps living things going, so the colder its gets, the slower an organism's chemistry works and the tougher it is to survive. This means that animals and plants need special adaptations to cope with the icy cold, desert-like conditions of regions such as the Arctic and Antarctic. For the polar bear – one of the few animals that lives all year round in the Arctic – those adaptations include a double fur coat and a thick layer of insulating blubber, allowing the bear to endure winter air temperatures that average –34°C. Other creatures have 'antifreeze' chemicals that prevent or control the formation of ice crystals inside their bodies. Some simply find refuge from the cold by sheltering in the snow.

ADAPTING TO COLD

ALL SEAL SPECIES HAVE ONE THING IN COMMON – A THICK LAYER OF FATTY BLUBBER THAT PROTECTS THEIR BODIES FROM THE COLD. It makes them ungainly on land, but for the species living in and around the Antarctic, it is a vital adaptation to keep them warm in the icy waters of the Southern Ocean.

Of the 35 species of living seal, six make the Antarctic and its waters their home – the crabeater, Ross, Weddell, leopard, southern elephant and Antarctic fur seals – and they occur in huge numbers. The Antarctic has more seals than the rest of the world combined, and after humans, crabeater seals are thought to be the most numerous large mammals on Earth, with an estimated population of 40 million individuals.

Warming blubber

Scientists working in the Antarctic have taken ultrasound scans of Weddell seals, which show that their blubber layer is 4–6 cm thick along the entire length of the body. Photographs taken with infrared cameras show that no heat at all is lost from the bulk of a seal's body; it only escapes through an open mouth, from the nostrils when a seal breathes out and from the linings of the eyes – surface blood vessels prevent the eyes from freezing up when Weddell seals are hunting under the ice.

LAZY AFTERNOON Crabeater seals rest on an iceberg near Pleneau Island off the Antarctic Peninsula. The seals haul out on average for about eight hours during the day. At night they dive in search of krill, their main food. A layer of blubber keeps them warm.

Some adaptations for the cold are in place from birth. Instead of having a blubber layer, newly born Weddell seal pups are kept warm by a thick coat of fur, known as lanugo, from the Latin word for 'woolly down'. (Human foetuses also have lanugo as a normal part of development, but it is shed in the womb before the baby is born.) In baby seals, unlike their parents, the ratio of body surface to volume is high, which means that even with fur, they could potentially lose heat rapidly. To avoid this, the pup's body does not direct blood to the skin. As pups grow, they put on blubber, lose the lanugo and start to regulate their body temperature in the same way as adult seals. By the time they are one month old, the pups already have a 4 cm layer of blubber.

Heat regulation

As well as the cold, Weddell seals have to deal with the heat when they haul out onto the ice on warm days in summer. They 'towel-dry' themselves in soft snow and lie around in the Sun for days on end. The danger now is that they might overheat, and one organ, in particular, has to be kept cool – if the male seal's testes reach too high a temperature, the sperm becomes less viable. Unlike male land mammals, whose testes are in an external scrotal sac, the male seal's testes are in a special compartment inside the body. A dense network of blood vessels around the sac takes cooled blood returning directly from the hind flippers, through which the seal loses excess heat. In female seals, a similar network of blood vessels regulates the temperature of the developing foetus.

If seals remain out on the ice for any length of time, their entire bodies radiate heat, not just the flippers. This is evident from the seal-shaped depressions they leave behind when they move, where the ice has melted. The heat is lost through bunches of highly branched arteries and veins under the skin that sit side by side with hair follicles. These act like thermal perforations in the skin for the heat to escape. If a snowstorm is whipped up by high winds and the temperature drops to –20°C, the seals drop back into the water where conditions are more stable. Here, blood is directed away from the skin and flippers, and the seals keep warm even when the sea temperature is close to freezing point.

WARM DOWN A red-breasted goose keeps her chicks warm on the Taimyr Peninsula in the Russian Arctic. For red-breasted geese, as for most birds, insulating feathers are the equivalent to a mammal's blubber. The geese need this kind of adaptation to the cold, because they nest when snow is still on the ground.

SURVIVING SUBZERO

FOR SOME LIVING ORGANISMS, THE FREEZING POINT OF WATER IS POSITIVELY WARM. For them, things get really cold only when the temperature plummets towards –50°C. When this happens, they opt out of living and lie dormant until conditions improve. A few organisms can survive like this for an extraordinarily long time. Scientists bringing up ice cores from deep in the Antarctic ice sheet have uncovered algae and fungi that must be tens to hundreds of thousands of years old, judging from the depth at which they were found in the ice, thousands of metres down. Yet the long-dormant organisms were brought back to life again.

Avoiding the freeze

In less extreme conditions, similar principles apply when animals, such as the North American red bat and big brown bat, hibernate during the winter. When hibernating, the bats are truly dormant: breathing is hardly perceptible, the heart rate drops from a normal 400 beats per minute to 25 and body temperature falls to within a few tenths of a degree of the air temperature in the place where they are hibernating – often a cave, the attic of a house, or an abandoned woodpecker nest. If the temperature falls below freezing, some stir from hibernation to raise their body temperature; others remain dormant, but the unconscious body still recognises the drop in temperature and increases its metabolism sufficiently to compensate.

When the temperature falls a long way below freezing point, the chief danger for living organisms is that ice crystals will form inside the body and kill them. If a creature is to survive extremes of cold, it needs to prevent this happening, which is why a number of fish, insects, plants and bacteria have 'ice-structuring' proteins and glycoproteins in their blood or tissues. Although often referred to as 'antifreeze' proteins, these do not work in the same way as the antifreeze in a car's cooling system, where a solvent is added that lowers the freezing point of the water in proportion to the concentration of solvent. Instead, the proteins bind to the surfaces of the ice crystals, modifying their size and shape and stopping them from growing. This enables fish, such as winter flounder, northern cod, sculpins, smelt and herring, to survive in water close to –1.9°C, the freezing point of seawater. In Antarctic fishes, such as the notothens (or rockcods), the antifreeze proteins are produced in the pancreas and stomach.

Some antifreeze proteins are more effective than others. In northern Asia, Europe and North America, the spruce budworm caterpillar and the mealworm beetle have 'hyperactive' antifreeze proteins that can control the direction in which ice crystals grow to make sure that they do not cause damage.

FREEZING BAT Hoar frost has formed on the fur of a Bechstein's bat (left) hibernating in a French cave. If the bat does not stir soon to raise its body temperature or move to a warmer place, it will die.

COLD FISH The emerald notothen (below) lives mainly on the Antarctic seabed, from the shallows down to depths of 700 m. It has 'antifreeze' proteins in its blood to prevent it from freezing.

Snow fleas – not, in fact, fleas, but a species of springtail that lives on snow and ice – have still more effective chemicals. Up to a hundred times more powerful than the chemicals in fish, these enable the snow fleas to survive in temperatures as low as −30°C. Scientists have isolated the compounds and use them, among other things, to preserve transplant organs at low temperatures without damage.

All these chemicals are known as 'freeze-avoidance' proteins. Another class consists of the 'freeze-tolerant' proteins. These enable organisms to freeze and then thaw without damage to their cells. Thanks to freeze-tolerant proteins, wood frogs and baby painted turtles are two of the very few vertebrates that can survive freezing of their tissues.

Plant antifreeze methods

Plants have weaker antifreeze proteins. One of only two flowering plants that grow on the Antarctic Peninsula is the Antarctic hair grass. This has proteins that do not prevent ice crystals forming, but stop them from re-crystallising so that the crystals remain extremely small and so do not harm the plant. The plant actually initiates the formation of tiny ice crystals by producing ice 'nucleators'. These attract water molecules, which then freeze at a slightly higher temperature than normal. In this way, the plant is in control of the way water freezes in and around its tissues.

Evergreen plants, such as conifers, avoid damage from freezing by shifting the water from inside their cells to the spaces between the cells. The water outside the cells freezes, while the more concentrated fluids inside, which contain sugars and other natural antifreeze chemicals, are less likely to freeze. This means that the biggest challenge for conifers in winter is not dark, cold days but the occasional calm, sunny and warm ones. As the leaves warm up, water vapour is lost and the tree is in danger from desiccation rather than freezing.

Sugars, salts, amino acids and other chemicals in solution can all act to 'supercool' water so that it freezes at a lower temperature than normal. To take advantage of this property, many over-wintering plants store such chemicals in their cells in autumn – the plants tend to 'harden up' in response to dropping temperatures, and this prompts them to accumulate the chemicals. Other plants overwinter as bulbs: the temperature underground rarely falls below −1°C, and sugars and starches stored in the bulbs lower the temperature at which any water content freezes. Other plants again die back each autumn and survive as dry seeds, which are immune to freezing. In the Sixty Mile River area of Klondike in North America, lupin seeds that had been frozen for more than 10 000 years inside ancient lemming burrows proved to be viable and grew into new plants.

Antarctic lichens

In the Antarctic, several species of lichen cope with the extreme cold, the rarest being the Antarctic lichen. Like all lichens, the Antarctic lichen is a product of a symbiotic relationship between an alga and a fungus, but its alga differs from those in other lichens because it can photosynthesise at a temperature of −20°C. The lichens of the Antarctic grow incredibly slowly, some no more than 1 cm per century, others by as little as 1 cm per millennium.

Another group of organisms that survive on the coldest continent are the cryptoendoliths, associations of algae and bacteria that live in minute cracks just below the surface of porous, semi-translucent sandstone. The see-through rock acts like a greenhouse, allowing in enough light and water for the cryptoendoliths to grow.

Elsewhere in the Antarctic, the only obvious green living things are green algae around mud puddles in spring and summer, which are covered by snow and ice throughout the winter. In some places, there are areas of snow that look blood-stained in summer because of a red alga that grows in them. This is found mainly near penguin rookeries, where organic material from penguin droppings has been blown onto the snow, providing fertiliser that helps the alga to grow.

LONG-LIVED SEEDS If seeds from these lupins in south-eastern Alaska become trapped in the nearby Mendenhall Glacier, they could remain in the glacier for hundreds of years and still be viable if and when the ice melts.

WOOD FROG

THE ONLY AMPHIBIAN LIVING NORTH OF THE ARCTIC CIRCLE IS THE NORTH AMERICAN WOOD FROG. Exposed in winter to some of the lowest temperatures on Earth, about half the wood frog's body freezes solid as it hibernates in the upper layer of the soil or under leaf litter. Flat ice crystals form underneath its skin and distribute themselves among its skeletal muscles. Eventually, the body cavity fills with ice, encasing all the internal organs. The frog's heart stops beating, breathing ceases and its eyes turn white because the lenses freeze.

The wood frog can tolerate freezing because it controls the process. Ice 'nucleators', which can be bacteria or proteins, actively seed ice crystals so that the frog freezes at a slightly higher temperature, just below 0°C, than it would do without the nucleators. The higher temperature means that the ice forms slowly, allowing the animal to make adjustments for its survival. Special proteins, glucose and urea (a compound also present in human urine) prevent water inside the cells from freezing or the frog from dehydrating. In this way, the frog's cells are safe, while the creature itself freezes solid.

In spring, the wood frogs thaw out and head for temporary meltwater ponds to reproduce. The temporary nature of the ponds gives them an advantage, as there are no predatory fish to eat the tadpoles. Having hibernated close to the ponds, they can reproduce immediately, giving the tadpoles time to develop before the ponds dry up in the summer.

VITAL STATISTICS

CLASS: Amphibia
ORDER: Anura
SPECIES: *Lithobates sylvaticus*
HABITAT: Woodlands, forested swamps and bogs
DISTRIBUTION: North America
KEY FEATURE: Survives partial freezing in winter. Ranges far and wide in summer when searching for food.

UNDER ICE

ICE IS ESSENTIAL FOR SOME ANIMALS. In the Arctic, the sea ice that forms in winter is the only place where polar bears can hunt their main prey, the ringed seal. The seals, which belong to the most numerous Arctic seal species, live below the sea ice, but being mammals they have to come to the surface to breathe. They have tiny breathing holes, just big enough for their nostrils to fit in, but still large enough to give away their position. A polar bear goes from hole to hole checking to see which one is being used and then waits. When a seal comes up, the bear pounces.

Larger holes in the Arctic ice, known as 'sassats' (the Inuit word for them), are sometimes the only access to air for belugas or white whales. The whales can get trapped under the ice, and when this happens they crowd around sassats, taking it in turn to surface and breathe. Polar bears stake out these holes, too. Even larger, permanent holes, called 'polynas' (another Inuit word), are kept open by strong currents. These attract whales and seals, but also birds, incuding eiders, which dive into the open waters to pick mussels from the seabed.

At the other end of the world, in shallow Antarctic waters, there are whole communities of seabed animals under the ice. Many of these animals are related to deep-sea creatures usually associated with other parts of the ocean floor. They include species of sea lily or crinoids – not plants, but relatives of sea urchins. Sea lilies are normally found in water that is 2000 m deep or more, but the Antarctic speces live at depths of less than 30 m.

Some of the seabed creatures are giants. There are Antarctic isopods (a type of crustacean), which resemble woodlice but are 17 cm long; shrimp-like creatures called amphipods, up to 10 cm long; huge sea spiders, which measure 33 cm across; ribbon worms that stretch for 3 m from head to tail; and sponges that are 3 m across. Paradoxically, these giants are the result of unusually slow growth in the cold seas. Low metabolic rates

STELLAR CARPET A population of pink sea stars, a species of starfish, lives under the Antarctic ice in less than 30 m of water. They feed on other starfish and on seal droppings left under seal breathing holes.

allow the animals to grow for longer than their relatives in temperate shallow seas. Their only threat comes from icebergs, which occasionally float in and wreak havoc as they move across the seabed, crushing entire communities with their weight.

Other inhabitants of these waters include sea cucumbers and starfish. Three-quarters of Antarctic fish species are notothens (see page 41). Of the others, the near-transparent ice fish is the most unusual. Its blood has little haemoglobin (the iron-containing protein that makes blood red), so the fish is colourless. Even, the parasitic leeches that live on the ice fish's body are colourless.

Lake life

In lakes that freeze over in winter, life becomes muted as the layers of ice and snow on top of them cut off the light and reduce photosynthesis by green water plants and algae. Phytoplankton levels drop and so food is generally scarce. Animals, such as frogs and terrapins, hibernate in the mud at the bottom of a lake. Microorganisms, such as rotifers and protozoans, form protective shells called cysts, inside which they lie dormant until the spring thaw. Adult water fleas die after producing thick-walled eggs that will survive until spring.

Larger lakes can turn topsy-turvy. In summer, the warmer water is at the top and the colder water at the bottom. In winter, the reverse sometimes happens – insulated from the cold air by the layers of water, ice and snow above it, the water at the bottom of the lake retains its warmth better. The ice and snow at the surface also insulates the lake from further freezing.

For beavers, which create their own ponds, ice presents no problem. When a beaver family's pond freezes over, the animals can still enter and leave their lodge of branches and mud through special underwater entrances below the ice. Before leaving the lodge, they elevate their body temperatures slightly so they can stay longer in the cold water.

CLAM DIGGER A walrus uses drifting pack ice as a raft to reach the clams on which it feeds. It uses the bristles of its moustache to find the shellfish and then squirts water from its mouth to uncover them.

SAFETY IN SNOW

IN WINTER MONTHS, IT IS OFTEN WARMER BELOW THE SNOW THAN IT IS ON TOP OF IT. To take advantage of this relative warmth, lemmings and voles create networks of tunnels through the snow, allowing them to remain active during the cold weather. In the Arctic, the collared lemming turns white for the winter and grows special claws on the third and fourth digit of each front paw. The claws, which it loses in spring, are effectively snow shovels, enabling the lemming to excavate its tunnels, along with multichambered burrows under the ground. Other adaptations for the cold include the lemming's stubby ears, legs and tail, all of which help it to retain heat.

While the temperature above the snow is well below freezing, down in the tunnels it can be a relatively comfortable 10°C. The tunnels also help lemmings to remain out of sight of predators, such as snowy owls, wolverines and Arctic foxes, although ermine or stoats are more of a threat, because they are slim enough to slip in and hunt inside the tunnels. The main problem is the build-up of carbon dioxide from the animals' breath. If this reaches danger level, the lemmings excavate another tunnel to the surface for fresh air. Small birds, such as redpolls, sometimes move in with the lemmings to shelter from the cold.

For food, the lemmings browse on grasses, sedges and bark from dwarf willow and dwarf birch. During the course of the winter, they will clip almost all the plants near their nest, but if these run out, they have seeds cached in storerooms in their burrows. They also carry on breeding through the winter – lemmings can have a litter of 12 almost every month of the year. With females that mature at only five weeks old, this means that when food is plentiful so are lemmings.

WINTER NIBBLER On Arctic Russia's Taimyr Peninsula, a collared lemming in winter colours has forsaken the safety of its snow tunnels to feed on dwarf willow. It has to be on the alert, because here in the open, it is in full view of predators, such as the snowy owl.

Birds in the snow

Like collared lemmings, ptarmigan or snow grouse change colour in winter. Their plumage turns white, apart from a black eye patch and tail, and the birds almost disappear from view when sitting in their 'snow roosts' – hollows or burrows they create in the snow. The feathers on their legs go right down to their feet, so there is little bare skin from which heat can escape.

In Canada, the ruffed grouse dives headlong into deep snow when landing. In this way, it digs out a roost that is just a little bigger than its body. The snow acts as a windbreak, reduces heat loss and to some extent insulates the bird. When in its snow den, the grouse will look out occasionally, especially if it hears a noise. If danger threatens, it lowers its head and reduces its heart rate so it can hear more clearly.

SNOW DEN If the snow is relatively shallow, the ruffed grouse sits with the lower part of its body in the snow and its head and neck exposed. This bird is roosting at Waterton Lakes National Park in Canada.

In Russia, willow ptarmigan have been known to remain in their snow dens for 21 hours a day, avoiding exposure to temperatures that drop to −40°C. To survive, the birds require about 60 g of food each day, mainly willow buds and twigs. Their muscular-walled gizzards are filled with small stones, which grind the food like grain in a mill. As winter progresses, the stones grind down to dust, and the birds have to find rocky outcrops, where the wind has blown the snow away, to get more stones to restock their gizzards.

Reindeer and moss

Wild caribou and domesticated reindeer (the same species) are well adapted to the snows of an Arctic or sub-Arctic winter. To deal with the scarcity of food in the snow-covered landscape, they simply reduce their need for it by lowering their metabolic rate. Even so, they still need to eat 9 kg a day, mostly reindeer moss – not a moss, but a species of ground lichen. They also feed on true mosses, wintergreen grasses and dwarf shrubs. The availability of these foods depends on snow cover. If the snow is not too deep, they use their broad, concave hooves to dig into it; deep snow sees them heading for forested areas where they feed on the lichens growing on trees. In the wild, caribou tend to vary their winter range from year to year in order not to overgraze areas.

In Arctic Canada, one insect, the snow scorpionfly, takes advantage of the winter to reproduce. It lives on foliage, such as mosses, hidden under the snow, and breeds not in spring and summer, like most other insects, but in the cold months when fewer of its predators are about. On warm days, the flies climb up through as much as a metre of snow and gather on the surface. They are just 6 mm long, with stilt-like legs that keep their bodies clear of the snow's surface. They mate and then climb back down again to the moss beneath, where they remain until the snow melts in spring.

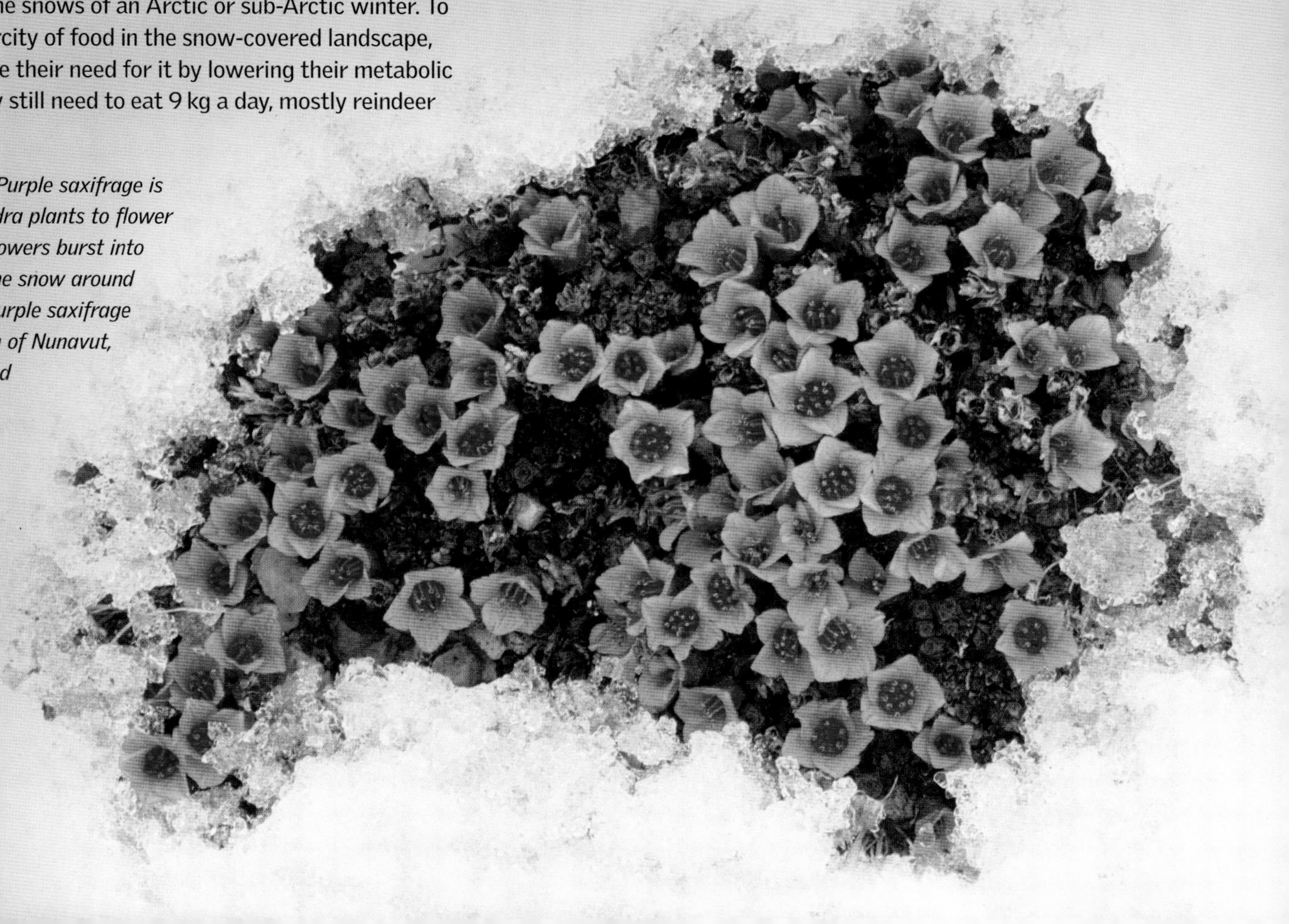

EARLY BLOOMER Purple saxifrage is one of the first tundra plants to flower in the Arctic. The flowers burst into bloom as soon as the snow around them has melted. Purple saxifrage is the floral emblem of Nunavut, Canada's largest and newest territory.

KEEPING WARM

EVEN IN SUBZERO TEMPERATURES, THE TINY NORTHERN WREN CAN SURVIVE THE COLD, maintaining its body temperature at a constant 40°C – a remarkable feat for so small a bird. The wren achieves this by converting food to heat, which means that it has to consume about a third of its body weight in food each day to survive. It is an insect-eater, but even in a snowy winter, it finds insects on bark and fallen logs. In hilly moorland areas, the wren disappears into the heather to forage, even when thick snow lies on the ground. Its roosts are in dark retreats, including the old nests of other birds.

When times get really tough, a family of wrens or several individuals will gather together – in North America, where the bird is known as the winter wren, a nest box in western Washington State was found to contain 31 individuals. This behaviour is not uncommon among animals. When the cold becomes intense, creatures that are normally solitary, such as the wren, huddle together for warmth. As many as 20 North American flying squirrels may pack into a section of hollow tree, while voles and deer mice build communal dens under the snow. The temperature outside may be –12°C, but inside the nest it is 10°C.

Small is warm

One of the most successful northern mammals is one of the smallest – the short-tailed shrew. It is a highly active creature, which takes 164 breaths a minute and has a heart rate of 760 beats per minute. To survive at this pace, the shrew must eat constantly. Living alone in an

SNOW BED AND FROSTED BLOSSOM *An Arctic fox (above) curls up in the snow on the shores of Hudson Bay, Canada. By hiding its nose beneath its tail, the fox leaves no naked surfaces from which it can lose heat. Its thick fur keeps it warm even in the worst blizzards. A frost-dusted bumblebee (below) settles on fireweed in Alaska. Queens are on the wing as soon as the snow melts and the willows blossom.*

underground nest, it has a network of tunnels under the snow in which to hunt for food, including insect pupae and larvae. Some of these it eats there and then; others it stores. The shrew has a venomous bite, which puts prey out of action but keeps it alive and fresh. To ensure that no other creature steals from the cache in its larder, the short-tailed shrew urinates and defecates over it.

The shrew has a second winter survival tactic – brown fat, a fatty body tissue often found in hibernating mammals as well as in newborn human babies. It accumulates brown fat in the area of its shoulder blades; as the fat breaks down, it generates heat. When the shrew feeds, it replenishes the fat store, making it one of the few animals that increases its weight in winter. The maximum store of fat occurs in mid-January, the coldest time of the year.

As many as 20 flying squirrels may pack into a section of hollow tree, while voles and deer mice build communal dens under the snow. The temperature outside may be –12°C, but inside the nest it is 10°C.

Early bees

Arctic summers are short, and a queen Arctic bumblebee cannot waste any time if she is to build a colony and bring up the next generation. As soon as the first flowers appear – usually purple saxifrage and willow – she is out looking for nest sites, often adopting the abandoned nests of lemmings and snow buntings. Some queens have been known to drive out snow buntings from their nests.

The queens are on the wing at a time of year when the air temperature would force any other flying insects into a deep torpor. For the bee's flight muscles to work, they need to be at a temperature of at least 30°C and preferably 35°C. The queens achieve this dramatic rise in muscle temperature, way above the air temperature, by shivering. This enables the bumblebees to forage both day and night, even with the mercury plummeting.

Arctic bumblebees – workers and drones as well as queens – also need to conserve heat. The workers and drones have a heat-exchange system in the thorax, which enables them to retain heat generated by the flight muscles while flying without pumping it to the abdomen. By contrast, the first queens to emerge have warm abdomens – at this stage, they pump warm blood from the thorax to the abdomen. They seem to be losing heat fast, but there is method in this apparent madness. The queens direct heat to their abdomens to incubate their ovaries and accelerate the development of the first eggs. Later, when a queen has established her nest, she has to keep the first brood warm – close to 32°C. She places her heated abdomen on the brood, like a nesting female bird keeps her eggs and chicks warm. In this way, she ensures that the temperature of the brood does not drop below 30°C, even when the air temperature outside is below freezing. Nectar from early flowering plants provides the fuel she needs to achieve this.

COLD FEET Swan geese in northern China redirect warm blood away from their feet to conserve heat. Their body temperature may be about 40°C, but their feet on the ice are close to zero.

INSULATION

MANY LARGE MAMMALS IN COLD CLIMATES HAVE AN EXTRA THICK FUR COAT IN WINTER, WHICH THEY THEN SHED IN SUMMER. The musk ox, for example, endures savage Arctic winter temperatures thanks to a thick double coat, consisting of a shaggy outer layer of long coarse hair, which covers the animal's entire body except its feet, and a soft, woolly undercoat. Size is one of the factors that allows the musk ox to get away with this kind of insulation. Being so large – a musk ox can weigh 400 kg or more and stand 1.4 m high at the shoulder – it is able to carry such a coat without being hampered in its movements. Among other mammals, larger creatures, including domestic dogs and cats, usually grow winter coats that are 3–7 cm thick. Smaller animals weighing less than a kilogram tend to have little change in pelt depth from summer to winter – for them, thick winter coats would simply be a hindrance, not a help.

Why white?

White fur or feathers are another adaptation to winter cold, found in animals such as white-tailed jackrabbits, Arctic hares, ermine and ptarmigan. This is something of a paradox, as a dark coat would absorb more heat, while a white coat reflects sunlight. Scientists have carried out experiments which show, for instance, that a Siberian hamster's white winter coat reflects 43 per cent of incoming sunlight, compared to 18 per cent when it has its brownish grey summer fur.

It was long believed that the chief reason for animals growing white coats or plumage in winter was camouflage, but scientists now believe that there could be another explanation – better insulation. With no pigment inside, the hair or feathers contain more air spaces. Even though more sunlight is reflected by a white coat, the air spaces make up for that by trapping warmer air and insulating the animal. This theory seems to offer a better explanation for the white winter coats of animals, such as the Arctic fox, that have no predators and so no great need of camouflage. A similar principle can be seen in polar bears, whose hairs are hollow and translucent. Although their fur appears white, this is just an optical illusion. The fur is colourless, while the skin beneath it is black to absorb heat.

Biologists are also reconsidering the cause of another phenomenon – the fact that weasels and related species, such as the martens, are larger the closer they live to the Arctic. Traditionally, this has been explained by the animals' need to store fat for the winter months or as a special adaptation to reduce heat loss, but a study of short-tailed weasels seems to point to a different conclusion. The size of short-tailed weasels increases the farther north they live, but the explanation could be simply that the northerly populations do not have to share a territory with the long-tailed weasel, the short-tailed's main competitor farther south. Without the rivalry, they feed better – the lack of competition rather than the pressure of cold weather may account for the size gain. All the same, the additional fat comes in handy when freezing weather sets in.

Whales, dolphins, seals and sea lions definitely do put on fat as insulation – enormous amounts of it. For water-dwelling mammals, thick fur would be less than useless, because wet fur loses 50 times more heat than dry fur. Thick layers of subcutaneous fat served by networks of blood vessels are far more effective. A 25 m long blue whale has a blubber layer, which is about 17 cm

thick on average and up to 30 cm thick in places. Killer whales have a blubber layer up to 10 cm thick. A 1.5 m long common porpoise has a blubber layer averaging 1.8 cm thick, going up to 3.6 cm thick behind the dorsal fin. Blubber in Arctic whales, such as the beluga, accounts for 40 per cent of the animal's body weight.

Feathered warmth

Penguins also have thick layers of fat beneath the skin, which allow the birds to hunt for days on end in the icy Southern Ocean. Among other birds, the snowy owl, like the ptarmigan, is an Arctic specialist with feathers that grow right down to its toes. When the temperature drops, it crouches on the ground, usually behind a rock or bush for protection from the wind.

Farther south, some birds, such as goldfinches and redpolls, grow more feathers in winter and fluff them out to insulate their tiny bodies. They have three types of feather: contour feathers, which have a downy component at their base; semi-plumes that are almost entirely downy; and down feathers. The outer contour feathers provide streamlining, while the downy feathers below trap an insulating layer of air. Erecting the feathers and increasing the layer of air makes for better insulation. Standing on one leg and tucking the beak under a wing reduces the amount of bare body surface from which heat is lost, while regulating the blood supply to the feet can also conserve heat. When it is very cold, birds shiver continuously to keep warm, producing more than five times as much heat as normal.

SNOW CAT A long, dense fur coat provides much-needed insulation for the magnificent snow leopard of the Himalayas. When the temperature plummets and blizzards blast its mountain home, the cat gets extra insulation from an unusually long tail, also covered with thick fur, which it wraps around its body, nose and mouth, rather like a scarf, to conserve heat.

EVERYDAY EXTREMES

COOL BIRD Temperature drops with altitude, so the Andean condor experiences extremes of temperature every day while soaring amongst the peaks and valleys of South American's great mountain chain.

A FEW ANIMALS EXPERIENCE BOTH HEAT AND COLD DURING THE COURSE OF A SINGLE DAY. A walrus, for example, swims in icy seas but then hauls out onto rocky beaches where the air temperature in summer can be upwards of 15°C. How does it cope with the contrast? The cold is no problem for the walrus, thanks to its ability to maintain different temperatures in its different layers of blubber and skin. The walrus's 15 cm thick blubber layer keeps its core body temperature at a steady 36.6°C, no matter what the surrounding temperature is, while the temperature in the skin layer varies – when the animal is swimming, this is no more than a few degrees above the water temperature. The insulation is so effective that when a walrus comes out of the water in winter, it can still function when the air temperature drops to –35°C. In summer, this could lead

to a problem of overheating, but the walrus has a way of dealing with that, too. When it is in the water, blood is shunted inwards away from the skin to minimise heat loss. When it hauls out, the blood is directed to the skin and the blood vessels dilate, so heat is lost.

Penguin beaches

At Punto Tombo on the coast of southern Argentina, tens of thousands of Magellanic penguins step out of the cold Atlantic onto beaches where the air temperature is considerably higher than the temperature in the sea. They are here to breed, but there is a danger of overheating. An anatomical adaptation that helps them to cope is a bare patch of skin above the eyes and bill from which heat can be lost. They share this with the three other temperate and tropical penguins – the Humboldt, Galápagos and African penguins. The penguins also try to find shade under bushes or in natural crevices, but if shade is unavailable they dig burrows up to a metre deep to shelter from the Sun. Other strategies include panting, standing in the wind, erecting their feathers to allow heat to escape from the skin below and holding out their flippers and directing blood into them – the flippers act as radiators that lose heat. If none of these is sufficient, the penguins can always go back to the cool water.

On South America's western side, Humboldt and Galápagos penguins live with exceptional extremes. Humboldt penguins swim in the cold Humboldt Current that sweeps up the continent's west coast, and they nest on the edge of the Atacama Desert. Galápagos penguins live on the Equator, hunting in water that is about 15°C, but nesting in areas where temperatures can reach 40°C. As a result, Galápagos penguins have less fat under the skin than other penguins, making them the smallest members of the penguin family. By contrast, the emperor penguin is the largest – essential for a bird that survives the rigours of the Antarctic winter, not in water but on land.

FACTS

ONE NORTH AMERICAN PLANT HAS ITS OWN HEATING system. The temperature of the skunk cabbage can be 20°C above the air temperature, enabling it to grow in the snow. To do this, the plant consumes the same amount of oxygen that keeps a hummingbird flying.

THE TINY, SLOW-GROWING ARCTIC WILLOW can live for 200 years or more. The world's northernmost woody plant, it grows close to the ground to avoid icy winds and its leaves have down-like hairs to prevent heat loss. It is a key food for a variety of animals from lemmings to caribou and musk oxen.

FACTS

COLOUR CHANGE Pacific walruses on a rocky beach on Round Island off Alaska. The blood directed to their skins to keep them cool has turned them pink. When the animals first emerge from the water, they are grey.

WETLAND WORLDS

3

THE SHALLOW, SALT-SATURATED WATERS OF LAKE NAKURU IN KENYA PRESENT A FORBIDDING HABITAT FOR MOST LIFEFORMS, but flamingos come here in their millions to feed on the blue–green algae that flourishes in the caustic environment. Around the world, plants and animals have colonised seemingly inhospitable wetlands. There are estuary specialists who cope with both fresh and seawater on a daily basis, and others that survive extremes of flood and drought. Birds such as the torrent duck are adapted to life in white-water rapids, while some fish have electric systems that enable them to negotiate dark and murky waters. Some opportunists, like this ambitious spotted hyena attempting to catch one of Lake Nakuru's flamingos, bridge the gap between wet and dry land in order to exploit a new source of food.

WHITE WATER

CRASHING DOWN OVER ROCKS AND GUSHING THROUGH STEEP-SIDED GORGES, the upper white-water sections of rivers look quite uninhabitable. And yet there are plants and animals that positively thrive in this turbulent environment that resembles the inside of a washing machine in action.

Creatures that live in such turbulent water have the benefit of high oxygen levels. Aquatic insect larvae, such as caddis fly larvae, live here, as long as they hang on tight. And where there is a source of food, there is usually something ready to eat it. Like the dipper, a short-tailed perching bird that lives and nests beside fast-flowing streams and rivers in North America and Eurasia. Named for its characteristic bobbing movement, the dipper feeds by walking or plunging into the white water and then scrambling along the stream bed. The dipper grasps rocks with its strong feet and then uses its wings to 'fly' momentarily underwater – a line of small bubbles revealing its course. While it is under the surface, it picks up caddis fly larvae and the larvae of beetles, freshwater limpets, shrimp-like amphipods, and even small fish. Underwater adaptations include dense plumage, a large preening gland to keep the feathers waterproof and nasal flaps to prevent water entering the bird's nostrils.

White-water ducks

The aptly named torrent duck nests in caves and crannies alongside white-water rivers flowing from the Andes, where it is perfectly at home in the turbulent waters. Holding a territory of around 1500 m, this powerful swimmer uses its long, stiff tail as a rudder underwater and as a support when standing on slippery rocks. The torrent duck dives below the surface to probe amongst the rocks for aquatic insect larvae, especially stonefly larvae, as well as mayfly larvae and molluscs.

The blue duck, or whio, of New Zealand is equally at ease in fast-flowing rivers, particularly rivers with steep gradients passing through upland forests. Like the torrent duck, the blue duck is extremely territorial – a mated pair will occupy the same territory for life and fiercely defend their patch of river against other ducks. Special protuberances known as 'metacarpal wing-knobs' on the bird's wings are used for fighting. Loss of habitat due to the clearance of forests close to rivers has caused the blue duck population to decline significantly. Predation by introduced animals, particularly stoats, is another factor.

DAREDEVIL DUCKS A pair of torrent ducks rests on rocks in the upper reaches of the fast-flowing Urubamba River near the ruins of Machu Picchu in Peru. The birds will vigorously defend this stretch of white water against any other ducks looking for a territory.

MAKING THE LEAP Salmon swim up the river of their birth in order to reach breeding sites in the headwaters. They go against the flow, slithering through rapids and leaping up waterfalls.

TIDAL ZONES

ESTUARIES MARK THE POINT WHERE RIVERS MEET THE SEA. They are important habitats for wildlife, but they are also a world of extremes. Here there are animals that live in mainly salt water with the incoming flood tide and mainly freshwater on the ebb. Everyday, they must adapt to each regime or die.

The main problem that estuary-dwellers have to contend with is a daily loss or gain of water caused by a natural process known as osmosis. Osmosis is the movement of water across a membrane or cell wall from an area of low-solute concentration (hypotonic) to an area of high-solute concentration (hypertonic). When in seawater, a marine organism is roughly the same concentration as the seawater, so it does not gain or lose water. But when it is in freshwater, the same marine organism can be considered an area of high concentration, so water will move into its body. In theory it would continue to enter until the creature bursts. So a marine animal living in an estuary must have a mechanism to lose water for at least half the day. A freshwater animal in an estuary, which has already adapted to living in freshwater, has the opposite problem. It is likely to lose water when the tide comes in and become dehydrated. For estuary animals the daily switch between fresh and saltwater poses a major water-regulation challenge.

One creature that copes with life between the two extremes is a tiny flatworm with the scientific name *Gunda*. It lives under stones on a pebbly beach in south Devon, where a freshwater stream pours into the sea. When the tide is out the flatworm is immersed completely in freshwater. When the tide is in it is surrounded by undiluted seawater. It is thought that calcium in the freshwater lowers the permeability of the flatworm's cells, so the creature takes in less water than would be expected by osmosis.

TUBE LIVING The peacock worm lives in a tough tube covered in particles of mud. Like exotic trees, the tubes stand proud of the substrate in which they are embedded. The fan of tentacles catches particles of food in the water.

Sharks out of saltwater

A rather larger creature that deals with the freshwater–saltwater problem, although not on a daily basis, is the bull or Zambezi shark. Adult sharks enter rivers from the sea and travel upstream, sometimes for long distances. They are mainly females, who enter freshwater to give birth to their pups. The reason they do this is that large sharks have a tendency to eat smaller sharks, no matter the species and they will even eat their own kind. The river affords a relatively safe haven away from most other adult sharks – the baby bull sharks only need to cope with a few crocodiles and inquisitive fish.

Moving between saltwater and freshwater is a major physiological challenge for these sharks, which retain high levels of the waste chemicals that other animals secrete. When they go into freshwater they must lower the osmotic gradient, that is reduce the amount of salts in their body to stop taking in water by osmosis. They do this by producing more urine and secreting salt from the rectal gland – failure to do so would result in them taking in so much water that their cells could rupture.

Bull sharks have been seen in many major rivers, including the Mississippi, Atchafalaya, Congo, Zambezi, Gambia, Tigris, Ganges, Hooghly, Mekong and Brisbane rivers. They have been known to attack hippos in the Zambezi, about 550 km from the estuary, and have been spotted 2800 km up the Mississippi River at Alton, Illinois. They have also been found an astonishing 3700 km from the sea in the Amazon River, which puts that shark in the middle of South America. In Central America they travel up the Rio San Juan to reach Lake Nicaragua. They are also found in Lake Ysabel in Guatemala and Lake Jamoer in New Guinea.

The bull shark is a hefty shark, reaching about 3.5 m long and weighing up to 230 kg, and it is considered to be one of the world's most dangerous sharks, responsible for many fatal attacks on humans. In 1916, for example, in an incident at Matawan Creek in New Jersey, five people were attacked and four of them killed within a space of a few hours of each other by a shark or sharks. At the time a great white shark was blamed, but three of the attacks occurred not in the sea but 5 km up a narrow tidal creek, a habitat where bull sharks might venture, but not great whites. Many scientists therefore believe a bull shark was responsible for the attacks.

RIVER CRUISE A bull shark swims in the River Sirena in Costa Rica. Unlike most other marine sharks, bull sharks tolerate freshwater.

River sharks

Along the coasts of southern Asia lives another group of freshwater-tolerant sharks, known as 'river sharks'. They inhabit brackish, freshwater and saltwater habitats, but unlike the bull shark, to which they are distantly related, they can survive where oxygen levels are low. Also unlike the bull shark, they are relatively harmless. One of them, the 2 m long Ganges River shark, was once considered a man-eater, but more recent research has shown that the attacks on humans had been made by bull sharks instead. Other river sharks are found in rivers in Malaysia, Burma, Borneo, New Guinea, and the Northern Territory and Queensland in Australia. Relatively little is known about them. The shape of their teeth indicates that they feed mainly on fish, and they have adapted to hunting in cloudy estuary and river waters. Hearing, smell and the detection of electrical activity in the muscles in prey are more important senses than sight.

The estuary floor

Estuaries are among the most productive places on Earth. With nutrients from both land and sea, they produce more food per hectare than a well-maintained field on an arable farm. They harbour a diverse range of habitats, including shellfish beds, sea-grass meadows, salt marshes and tidal flats, which are all home to many different species. There are ragworms, lugworms and cockles that burrow into the mud or scavenge over its surface. Oysters, clams and mussels blanket the estuary floor, where they are preyed on by boring sponges and predatory shellfish, such as oyster drills. Crabs, such as New Zealand's stalk-eyed mud crab and tunnelling mud crab, sift detritus from the water. If danger threatens they scuttle away into tunnels that

ON THE LOOKOUT The stalk-eyed mud crab is a resident of the intertidal mudflats of New Zealand, where it makes extensive burrows. The crab gets its name from its long, stalked eyes, which enable it to look about even when its body is hidden under mud or sand.

riddle the surface of the mud. The hairy-handed crab – named for the two hairy pads on the inner and under sides of its nippers – hides under rocks and seaweeds, using its pads to catch particles of food, such as diatoms. These crabs can be plentiful in the right conditions – in one New Zealand estuary, scientists counted 255 per square metre.

Estuaries are also home to fish, such as juvenile sea bass, dabs, flounders and grey mullet, which swim over the mudflats on the incoming tide, searching for shellfish and worms. On North America's east coast, the black drum fish has such a powerful bite it can crush an oyster shell. The same estuaries are the feeding ground of the horseshoe crab, a so-called 'living fossil' that is not a crab at all but a marine relative of spiders and scorpions; it has changed little in shape since ancient horseshoe crabs lived in Ordovician seas some 445 million years ago. It eats worms and molluscs, which it catches with small pincers on either side of its mouth.

At low tide, mudflats are a magnet for many species of shorebirds and waders, each with their own food preferences. Curlews and godwits use their long bills to delve deep into burrows to extract worms. Sanderlings follow the incoming tide, picking off food from the water surface. Oystercatchers use their strong bill to smash or pry open mussels, while turnstones, as their name suggests, literally turn stones over to get at the invertebrates hiding underneath.

All of these creatures are influenced by the coming and going of the tides, but those living in the water not only experience changes in salinity, but also changes in water level. On beaches and mudflats, the water disappears completely for part of the day and those that live here must have a survival strategy. Worms remain under the mud, while crabs disappear down burrows or hide under rocks or seaweed. As there is little or no oxygen in the mud, many mud-dwellers breathe through tubes to obtain oxygen from the surface.

Estuary plants

Many of the plants that grow in estuaries, especially those in salt marshes, resemble desert plants with fleshy leaves. They may be surrounded by water, but using it is a challenge. Because seawater has a higher concentration of salts than plant cells, most plants would lose water by osmosis. Salt-marsh plants avoid this by accumulating salt from the saltwater in their roots. When the concentration is high enough they take in water. Nevertheless, they have fleshy leaves with thick, waxy cuticles to limit their water loss. In Europe, glasswort is a typical plant of salt marshes, with fleshy leaves giving it the appearance of a cactus. It lives right on the waterline by storing the sodium it absorbs from the water into its tissues. From the 16th century, soda ash derived from the plant was used to make glass – hence the plant's common name. Further up the shore, where the land is not inundated by the sea every day, cord grass and sea purslane grow. Higher again are the flowering sea lavenders and sea asters.

To the sea and back

Some fish, such as salmon and common eels, divide their life cycle between freshwater and seawater. The salmon of the Pacific and Atlantic oceans start out in salmon redds – gravel nests – in the headwaters of rivers. They undergo several changes before heading for the sea. First they are hatchlings or alevins, which feed from a yolk sac and develop into fry. The fry grow into parr, which undergo a transformation to equip them for life in seawater, when they become smolt. The smolt have special chloride cells in their gills that pump out salts. They also develop silvery scales that prevent salt entering through the skin. The young salmon then make their way downstream to the estuary to acclimatise to saltwater before heading out to sea to feed and grow. On reaching maturity, they return, probably using an internal magnetic compass, to find the mouth of the river where they were born. At the estuary they pause to adjust to freshwater, secreting large quantities of mucous on the skin and gill filaments to prevent salts from escaping and water from entering. The number of special cells in their gills decreases. The salmon then use the sense of smell to find their way upstream. Many fail to make the transition and die and many more perish in waterfalls and rapids along the way. The rest push on to spawn upstream, after which many of the adults die.

The eel's life cycle works in reverse. The adult develops in freshwater and when ready to breed it drifts downstream to the sea. Like the salmon, it changes from a faintly yellowish colour to silver, and its skin thickens. Chloride cells in its gills pump out salts. Its eyes change colour from red to golden due to a special visual pigment that helps the eel to see in the low light of the deep sea. At low tide, it makes its way to the open sea. European and American eels head for the Sargasso Sea, an area of relatively still water in the middle of the North Atlantic Ocean, where they spawn and die. The eggs hatch and the leaf-like larva drifts in the ocean current, gradually transforming into an elver by the time it reaches its estuary. The elver is covered in mucous and heads upstream to lakes and rivers, where it grows and develops into an adult eel.

For salmon and eels this adaptation to saltwater and freshwater is a gradual process, but killifish, such as the mummichog that lives in estuaries and salt marshes on the North American east coast, are able to adapt rapidly to daily changes in salinity. They maintain the chloride cells in their gills throughout their lives. These small fish can also surivive in polluted water with low levels of oxygen. In 1973, a mummichog became the first fish in space when it was part of a biological experiment carried out on Skylab 3.

GLASS EELS The elver stage of the common eel's life cycle moves from the sea into the river. Elvers not only swim, but also wriggle over damp rocks to fight their way upstream.

CLOUDY HORIZONS

EACH YEAR, THE MIGHTY AMAZON RIVER CARRIES OVER 250 MILLION TONNES OF SILT FROM THE SOUTH AMERICAN CONTINENT DOWN TO THE SEA. At the river's 320 km wide mouth, its waters pour out at a rate of 175 000 cubic metres per second – ten times the discharge of the Mississippi River. A massive plume of sediment extends out into the Atlantic Ocean, forming a vast sand and mudbank 680 km long, 250 km wide and 11 000 m thick. Such a volume of sediment means that the animals in the Amazon River live immersed in an eternal 'fog' of clay and mud particles. Visibility is almost nil, so most of the 2500 species of fish have to feel their way in the gloom, and some have ingenious ways of doing this.

Weakly electric fishes

Beneath 'floating meadows' – rafts of vegetation that the river has torn from its banks and carries downstream – live fish that find their way in the cloudy water with the help of an electro-reception system. Known as 'weakly electric fishes', they have modified muscle or nerve cells that generate pulse-type electrical signals of up to one volt, plus an array of electrical receptors under the skin that detect electrical signals. Each fish produces a continuous stream of electrical pulses, surrounding itself by an electric field with a range of about one body length. When an object, whether an obstacle or another organism, moves within range it distorts the electrical field, and this is picked up by the fish's electro-receptors. It is a bit like a shadow falling on the fish's skin, and the darkness and fuzziness of the shadow indicate how far away the object is. The electrical properties of the object enable the fish to decide whether to approach, escape or ignore it. If the object produces its own electrical signals, such as the electrical activity of muscles, the weakly electric fish will pick this up, a useful sense to have when homing in on small prey animals, such as water fleas.

Weakly electric fishes also use their electrical system to communicate with others of their own kind. Each species produces different signals and has its electrical organs in different places on the body so it can identify a potential mate or rival. Females can establish whether a male is healthy and would make a good father simply by the signals he produces. The males of an African species of weakly electric fish use sounds to attract a mate but not before detecting the signals of her 'female' electrical field.

Shock tactics

The electric eel is capable of generating a much stronger electric charge, on average 500 volts and 1 ampere of current. It uses this power both to defend itself and to knock out prey – a shock from an electric eel is strong enough to cause serious injury to a human adult. Two of the eel's electric organs – the main organ and Hunter's organ – generate this high-voltage electricity. Their structure is similar to a car battery in which stacked plates create a charge, and they take up over half the electric eel's body. The third organ – the Sach's organ – produces less powerful pulses,

LITTLE SHOCKER The elephant-trunk mormyrid is a weakly electric fish from the Congo and Cameroon. It feeds on small invertebrates buried in the mud. Its long snout is studded with touch and taste sensors.

FACTS

THE WEAKLY ELECTRIC male African elephant fish courts the female with a sound-based signal, but he will wait for her to return a female electric organ discharge (EOD) before he makes a move.

WHEN ATTACKING prey, an electric eel disharges many thousands of pulses of high-voltage electricity.

IN 2005, FISHERMEN in northern Thailand caught a 2.7 m long Mekong catfish weighing 293 kg. It took them over an hour to haul it in, the largest freshwater fish ever caught.

FACTS

at 10 volts and a frequency of 25 Hz, which the eel uses in echolocation to navigate its way around, locate prey and find a mate. The electric eel, which is not a true eel but related to the knife fish, lives mainly in the murky rivers of the Amazon and Orinoco basins. It feeds on fish and small mammals, which it zaps with its powerful electric charge.

Fish with feeling

Many catfish get around in murky rivers with the help of barbels on their head. These resemble cat-like whiskers, and they work as feelers to detect food. There can be up to four pairs of barbels – one pair on either side of each nostril, a pair on either side of the mouth and another pair on the chin. Different species have different combinations, and some have none at all. Catfish tend to live on the river or lake bottom, where they eat detritus, carrion, worms, water snails and other fish. Larger catfish, such as the European wels, also take ducks and other animals from the surface.

EUROPEAN GIANT The European wels catfish grows over 2 m long and weighs up to 220 kg. Two long barbels on the upper jaw and four short barbels on the lower jaw are used to locate food, such as worms, snails and fish.

DRYING OUT

EVERY FEW YEARS MONSOON RAINS FILL LAKE EYRE, LOCATED IN THE DRY OUTBACK OF CENTRAL AUSTRALIA. It is more usually a dusty, iron-red desert with sparse, dull-green vegetation of lignan, hopbush, mulga shrubs and eucalyptus. But when the rains fall and the lake begins to fill there is a sudden rush of activity. As if by magic, birds appear in the desert in huge numbers – not desert birds but seabirds and waders. Six to eight million water birds, representing over 60 known species, descend on the lake from places hundreds of kilometres away. Some, such as white pelicans, cormorants and silver gulls, fly all the way from the south coast near Adelaide. Avocets, banded stilts, and whiskered and gull-billed terns join them. How they know, at such distance, that the lake has filled is a mystery.

With the arrival of water, plants such as ruppia and cane grass, water primrose and milfoil burst into flower. Blue-green and green algae blooms provide a superabundance of food for small invertebrates. Biting midges, water fleas, mosquitoes, water beetles, copepods and fairy shrimps appear overnight. From just a 20 cm square patch of lakebed tens of hundreds of tiny invertebrates emerge. Fish such as bony bream and hardyheads move in from other more permanent bodies of water, which during the flood are interconnected, albeit briefly. The fish are tolerant of extremes of conditions. Most can survive in water at a temperature of 35°C. Desert gobies and spangled perch can tolerate 42°C and low oxygen levels.

Every living thing is in a frantic race to complete its breeding cycle before the water in Lake Eyre disappears once

MUD PROBING A pair of marabou storks use their huge meat-cleaver bills to hunt for catfish trapped in a drying pool in the Masai Mara Game Reserve, Kenya.

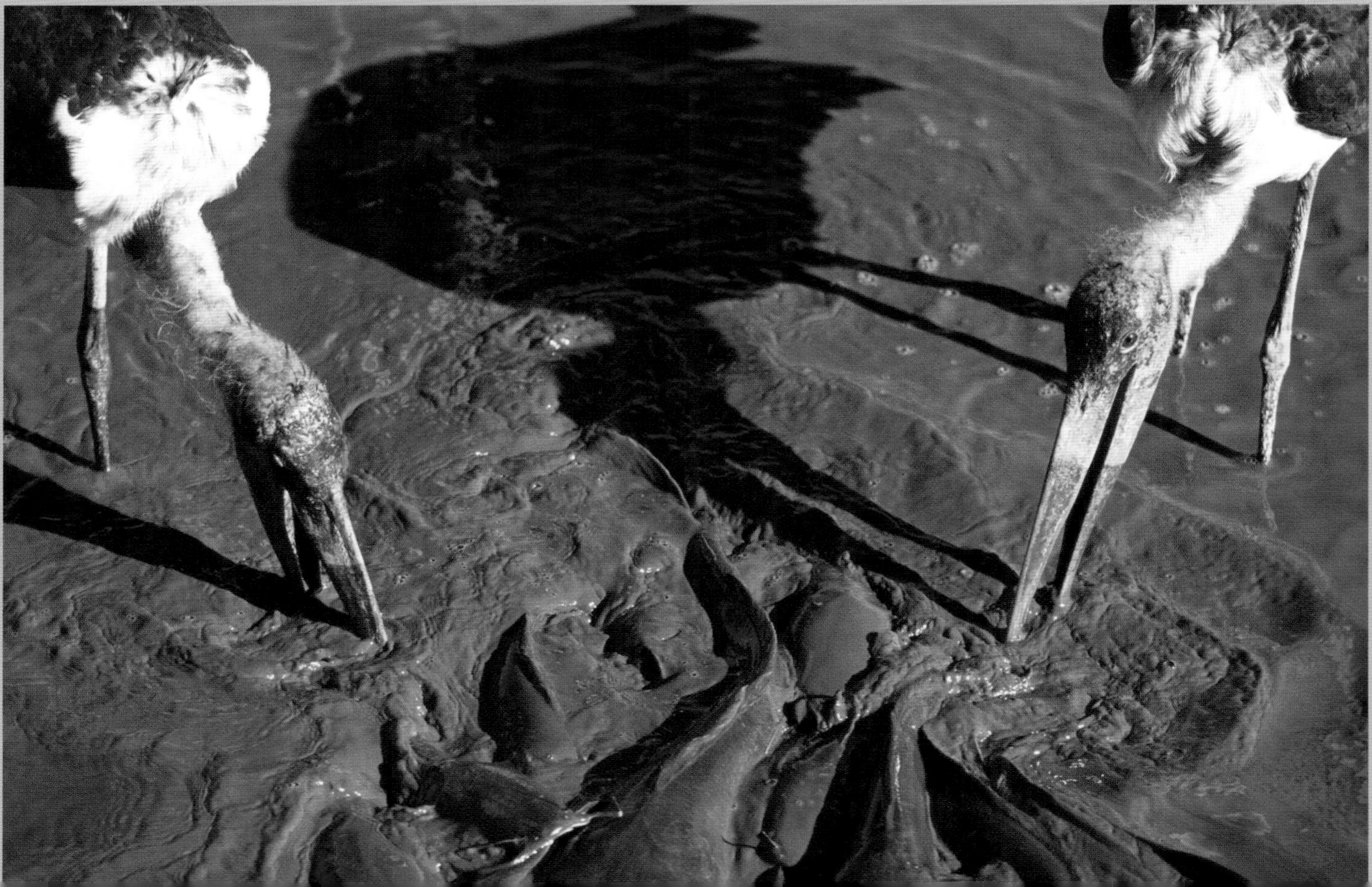

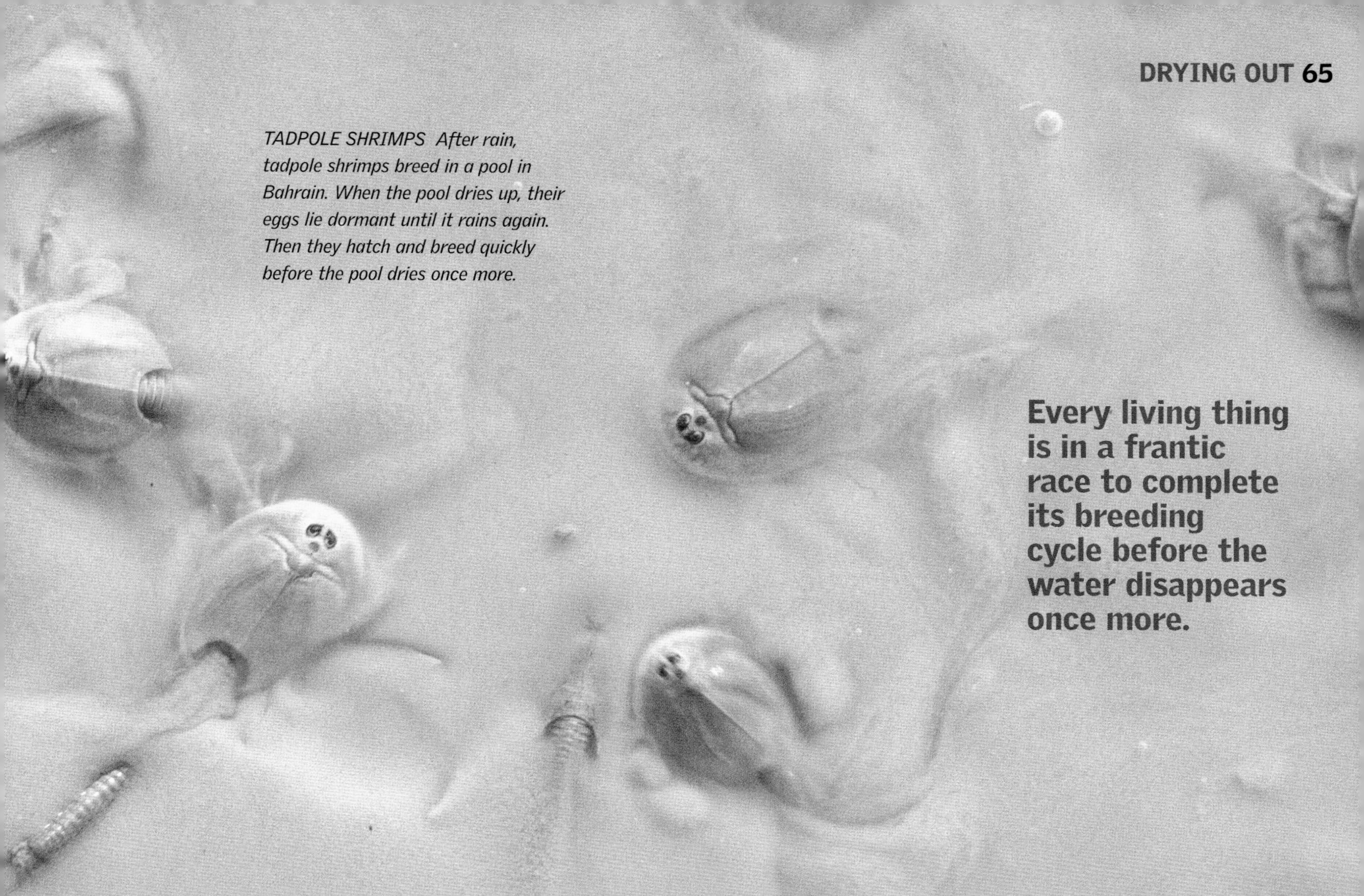

TADPOLE SHRIMPS After rain, tadpole shrimps breed in a pool in Bahrain. When the pool dries up, their eggs lie dormant until it rains again. Then they hatch and breed quickly before the pool dries once more.

Every living thing is in a frantic race to complete its breeding cycle before the water disappears once more.

more. Brine shrimps and shield shrimps need no more than two weeks to produce the next generation, trilling frogs fours weeks. Small fish, such as hardyheads, rainbowfish and glass perches, play safe and deposit 20 to 60 eggs each day. Large fish, such as catfish, grunters and perches, lay masses of small eggs. Some aquatic invertebrates deposit two types of egg, one when it is wet and a drought-resistant egg, no bigger than a grain of sand, when it is drying out.

In temperatures that frequently hit 50°C, the water evaporates or disappears underground and the birds leave. Residual ponds can be 10 times saltier than the sea and any fish that have not migrated back to more permanent areas of water will die. The water-holding frog stores water in its bladder and burrows under the lakebed. Water snails seal the opening of their shells with a thick cover and become dormant. Plants produce seeds that resist desiccation. Every living thing prepares itself for the long drought, but is ready to burst into life the moment the waters return.

Amazon boom-and-bust

The Amazon Basin may be one of the wettest places on Earth, but there are times when its river creatures have to cope with desert conditions. For part of the year, the Amazon River and its major tributaries overflow into the adjacent forest – the 'flooded forest'. River dolphins swim in the treetops and fish eat nuts. It is a topsy-turvy world, but during the other part of the year, the water level drops and freshwater sponges festoon branches that were once submerged. The sponge produces drought-resistant reproductive bodies, called gemmules, and these survive until the waters come back. Bivalve molluscs bury themselves in the ground, their bodies barely ticking over. Oxbow lakes shrink and the fish in them are concentrated in huge numbers in the liquid mud. The local spectacled caiman are guaranteed a catch every time: all they need to do is open their mouths, make a shallow pounce and clap their jaws shut. Egrets and cormorants fly in to join the feast, with flocks so large they blot out the Sun. Many fish die, but the traíra can survive in just a few centimetres of water by using its modified swim bladder as lungs to breathe air. It hides in shallow pools and intercepts anything that passes by, making these pools off-limits for frogs.

For the Amazon's giant river turtles, drying out enables them to breed, just as their ancestors have done for the past 60 million years. For the world's largest freshwater turtles – measuring up to 1 m across and weighing nearly 50 kg – the drop in water level means that the sandbanks on which they dig their nests are now positioned in the middle of the river. For two weeks prior to egg-laying, the females haul themselves onto the sand and bask in the sunshine for up to eight hours a day. The sun's warmth helps to speed up the development of the eggs inside them. By mid-morning, turtles are stretched out four or five deep like sunbathers on a crowded beach. Then, they begin to dig their nests, turning the once pristine sand into something resembling a war zone. Each

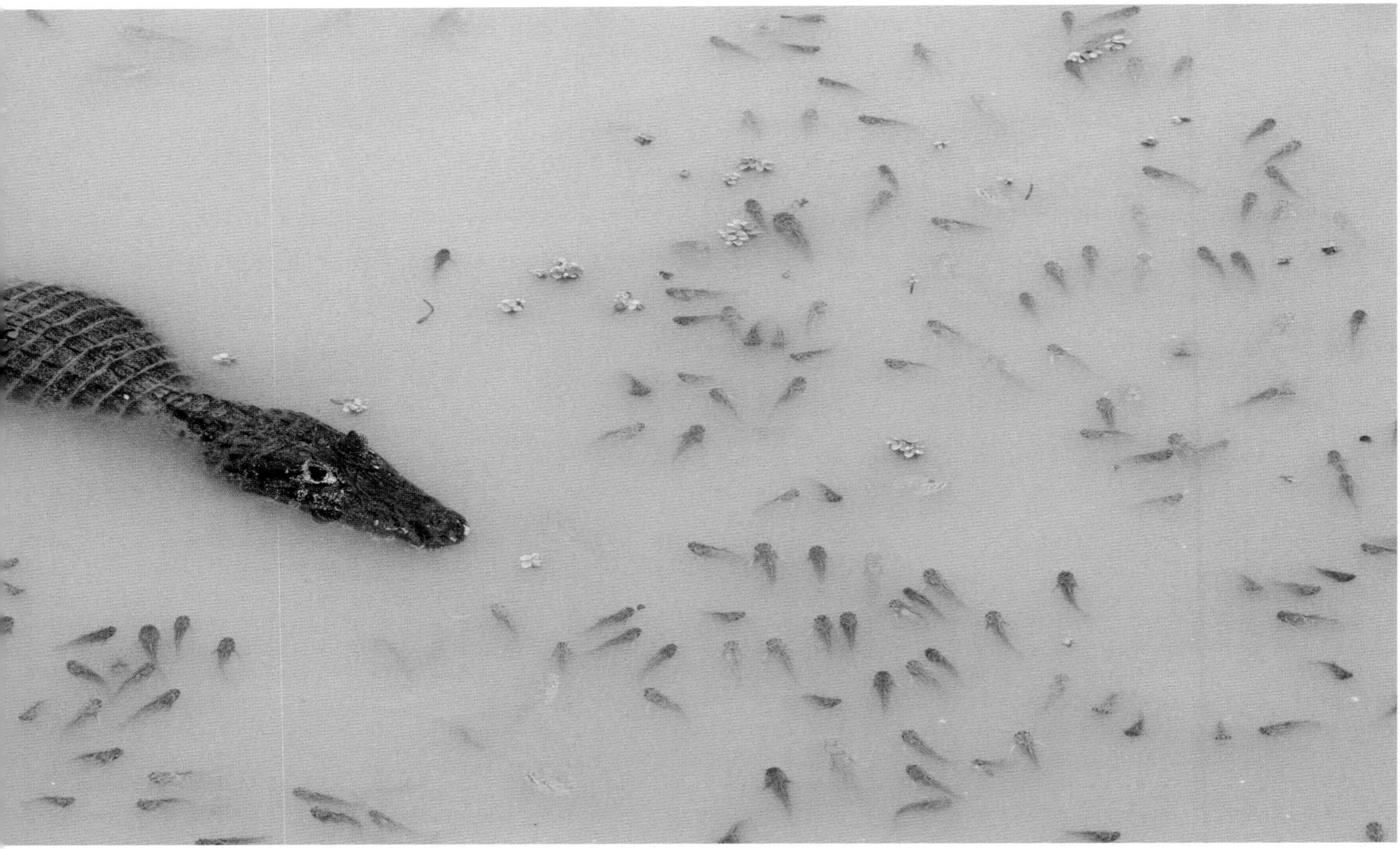

GOOD FISHING A shrinking waterway in Brazil's Pantanal wetlands makes fishing easy for a jacaré, or southern spectacled caiman. As the water level drops, the fish become more densely packed.

female turtle digs a hole in which she drops up to 130 eggs. On an overcrowded beach, previously laid eggs can be inadvertently dug up and black vultures wait to swoop on any eggs that are exposed. For those that survive, it is a race against time: the young turtles must develop, hatch out and be gone before the river begins to rise and the sandbank is covered in water once again.

African drought

The desert elephants of the Namib along Africa's south-west coast may be well adapted to living in hot, dry conditions, but they are constantly searching for water. One day a mud wallow is liquid, the next it is as solid as concrete. In times of drought, the water still flows, but deep under the desert sand. Although desert elephants can survive several days without water, they generally consume up to 230 litres a day. To survive, desert elephants embark on sometimes epic migrations in pursuit of water. It is the eldest elephant – the matriarch – that knows where water is to be found. Using a kind of ecological memory, she leads the herd along paths across the desert, sometimes travelling in the blazing Sun for 50 km between waterholes. The herd's home range might encompass 3000 km^2 of desert and scrub, and water sources are so spread out some are visited only once a year. The very survival of the elephants depends on knowledge of these sparse drinking sites. If there is no water on the surface, they use their trunks to dig down several metres and they have an uncanny knack of digging in the right place to find water. Nobody knows how.

During a bad drought in 1981, when 85 per cent of desert-adapted animals in the Namib, such as gemsbok and springbok, died of starvation and dehydration, the elephants expanded their range even more. They visited water sources seldom visited in normal years, much further away from their regular migration paths. All the elephants survived.

During an extended period of drought in East Africa, the savannah elephants slake their thirst by ripping open the trunks of baobab trees and drinking the water inside. A single elephant might knock over or rip apart about 1000 trees a year.

Drought can also give rise to bushfires set alight by lightning strikes. Most animals are adapted to cope. Small mammals and larger invertebrates hide in burrows and tunnels, birds and large mammals flee from the flames. But there is one bird that flies towards the fire. The flames attract the fork-tailed drongo: it feasts on any insects flying from the flames and picks up any that were roasted in the fire.

LUNGFISH

THE AFRICAN LUNGFISH IS A LIVING, BREATHING REMINDER OF WHAT FOUR-LEGGED VERTEBRATES

(tetrapods) might have looked like when they first emerged from the water and began to conquer the land some 360 million years ago. The lungfish is not a tetrapod, it is a fish and has gills, but it also breathes air through a modified swim bladder. It cannot walk but its fleshy pectoral and pelvic fins resemble legs. The lungfish has the body of an eel-like fish, with a flexible skeleton – if caught it can twist into a C-shape, then shoot off in any direction. Instead of a vertebral column, it has a notochord, a primitive feature more usually found in vertebrate embryos rather than adult animals.

Today, African lungfish live in the shallow waters of swamps and marshes and in lakes, such as Lake Victoria. Many live in places where the water disappears seasonally, but this is not a disaster for the lungfish. It burrows into the bottom sediments while they are still soft, and secretes a mucous cocoon around itself in which it can survive drought. The mud may be as hard as concrete, but the lungfish is safe inside its mucous-lined chamber until the rains come once more. It can remain incarcerated in this way for several months, its body ticking over at one-sixtieth of its normal metabolic rate. Other lungfish live in Australia and South America. All are difficult to age but specimens in zoos and aquaria have lived for 50 years or more. One in Shedd Aquarium, Chicago, is at least 65 years old. Fossil lungfish similar to modern specimens have been unearthed in fossil burrows in rocks 250 million years old. The oldest-known fossil lungfish was discovered in Yunnan, China, in rocks 410 million years old. The prehistoric creature differed from modern lungfishes in living in the deep sea.

VITAL STATISTICS

CLASS: Sarcopterygii
ORDER: Lepidosireniformes
SPECIES: *Protopterus annectens*
SIZE: Up to 2 m in length
HABITAT: Swamps and lakes
DISTRIBUTION: East, West and Southern Africa
KEY FEATURE: Can survive out of water for months.

MANGROVES

MANGROVES ARE TREES AND SHRUBS THAT GROW ALONG SHELTERED COASTS AND ESTUARIES IN THE TROPICS AND SUBTROPICS. They are adapted to live in water with high salinity and low oxygen, where the hot Sun beats down and the tide inundates the forest twice every day.

Red mangroves grow closest to the sea, propped up by stilt roots that take in air through pores in their bark. The perpetually waterlogged soil has little oxygen so these special structures help the plants with the process of exchanging oxygen and carbon dioxide. Red mangroves have tough roots that limit the uptake of salt. Any salt that does get through is directed to old leaves and lost when the leaves drop. White mangroves deal with salt in a different way – they excrete salt directly from salt glands at the base of each leaf. Their leaves are often covered with salt crystals, hence the common name. Black mangroves are found growing in more inland areas. They have special root-like structures lined with breathing pores that stick up above the surface of the mud from 30 cm to 3 m, depending on the species.

Propagation among the mangroves

Mangroves also have special adaptations for the survival of their offspring. Many seeds germinate while the seed is still on the parent tree, growing within or through the fruit. When this elongated 'propagule' is mature, it drops from the parent and floats away on

When it reaches suitable land, the mangrove propagule changes its density and floats vertically. If it fails to take root, it can change again and float away horizontally for a second attempt.

MARINE NURSERY Baby saltwater crocodiles pass their formative years among mangrove roots. They can grow up to be 6 m long, the world's largest living reptiles.

TREE SNAKE The 1 m long venomous mangrove viper is a nocturnal hunter. Heat sensors on its face detect prey such as birds and lizards.

the tide. It resists desiccation and remains dormant for up to a year. When it reaches suitable land, the propagule changes its density and floats vertically. If it fails to take root, it can change again and float away horizontally for a second attempt.

As long as mangrove crabs do not eat the seedlings, the mangroves become established and festooned with oysters and other shellfish. These serve to slow down water flow and encourage more sediment to settle. Mangrove crabs mulch any fallen leaves, thus increasing the amount of nutrients available for plants and animals. Myriad creatures move in – barnacles, sponges, bryozoans and various species of shellfish, together with mudskippers and fiddler crabs. But above all, mangroves are nurseries for a multitude of marine creatures, big and small. In the Caribbean, lemon shark pups spend their first few years in the mangroves, each pup having its own territory in which it feeds on smaller fry, with a particular penchant for baby octopuses.

SALT LAKES

HIGH IN THE ANDES OF SOUTH AMERICA, WATER FROM MELTING SNOW AND RAIN IS CHANNELLED INTO SALT LAKES, OR SALARS. Blue, green, pink, cloudy white and multicoloured – these high salt lakes come in a rainbow of colours depending on which bacteria and diatoms (algae) are living in them. Flamingos are one of the few birds that can take advantage of such a caustic habitat. Their enormous breeding areas are at the centre of these vast salt pans, which can be more than 10 000 km^2. The surface is a caked layer of painfully bright caustic mud overlying a deep muddy layer of grey ooze. The birds wade in with their long legs, then feed with their heads upside down between their legs. They filter diatoms and shrimps from the water by passing them from one side of their bill to the other, using their tongue as a pump: a mesh of plates, similar to a whale's baleen, filters out the food.

FOOD FIGHT At Lake Nakuru in Kenya, an African fish eagle has to defend its kill, a flamingo, from marabou storks who are trying to steal the remains of the carcass.

Thousands of flamingos arrive each South American spring to court and nest, their heads turning this way and that in a well-regimented courtship display. The female lays a single large egg in a nest of mud, built up off the lake floor to protect the egg and chick from any danger of flooding. By mid-summer crèches of baby flamingos stain the caustic mud with patches of grey. There is no shade or drinking water and daytime temperatures reach up to 60°C, so few predators venture out here – just the occasional culpeo fox in the cool of night.

Wet-season rains sometimes flood the pans to a depth of 2 m, but there are islands

of dark igneous rock that push up through the sea of salt and pools of brine. Here grow forests of candelabra cacti, their flowers attracting giant hummingbirds and sierra-finches. Viscachas, chinchilla-like rodents, scamper over the rocks, and puna hawks and Andean mountain cats try to catch them. Most lakes are shallow, and at these high altitudes their waters evaporate rapidly, concentrating the salts. They form high salt deserts, such as the Salar de Uyuni and Salar de Atacama, two of the largest salt pans in the world.

The salt layers are not flat, but resemble a ploughed field with small salt caverns and crevices. Small iguanid lizards live here, darting out of their hideaways to pluck flies from the enormous swarms that frequent the layer of still air a few millimetres above the salt. Sharing this unforgiving habitat is a mouse with a penchant for lizards. It is no more than 15 cm long, yet once it sinks its teeth into a 20 cm lizard, it does not release its grip. The two tumble between the runnels of salt until the lizard is dead.

HOT SPRINGS

The Devil's Hole pupfish has just one natural habitat – a geothermal (warm water) pool in a limestone cave in the Amargosa Desert to the east of Death Valley, Nevada. In winter, when the algae on which the fish feed is in short supply, the small population declines, but it picks up again in spring and summer. Nevertheless, as of 2007 there were only 42 of these small iridescent blue fish remaining at Devil's Hole. Some fish have been moved to aquaria, including one in a casino in Las Vegas, that replicate the fish's preferred conditions, in an attempt to ensure the survival of this unique species.

Great Rift Valley lakes

At Lake Nakuru, a strongly alkaline lake in Kenya, East Africa, more than a million lesser and greater flamingos come to feed on the blooms of blue-green algae (cyanobacteria) that thrive in the soda waters. Each year, a hectare of lake surface yields 250 000 tonnes of the algae, which is consumed by the birds. Sometimes there are so many birds that the surface of the lake becomes a seething mass of pink. The flamingos, in turn, are the targets for predators that watch and wait for the ill and infirm. African fish eagles swoop in to knock birds down, and marabou storks try to steal their prey. Black-backed jackals and spotted hyenas wade into the shallows to try their luck, sometimes catching a flamingo unawares. On another of the Rift Valley lakes, Lake Bogoria, hungry olive baboons crash into the dense flocks of flamingos bathing in freshwater, spicing their normally vegetarian diet with a little meat. This new taste for flamingo is having a visible effect on the baboons: the pigments in the birds' food that makes their feathers pink is also turning the baboons' normally greyish-brown fur to a lighter tan colour.

Lake Nakuru also attracts specialised fish-eaters. Along with the fish eagles, pelicans and cormorants come to the lake to catch a species of tilapia, a fish adapted to warm, alkaline waters that was introduced to combat mosquito breeding.

In recent years, Lake Nakuru has lost two-thirds of its water in drought, and pollution from local towns and factories is more concentrated in the lesser volume of water. As a consequence, some of the birds have moved on and flown to other soda lakes in the Rift Valley, where conditions are more conducive to flamingos. This mass exodus has occurred before in times of drought, but when the lake fills with water once more somehow the birds know and return to feed.

MORNING MIST At peak times there are between one and two million lesser flamingos at Lake Nakuru.

LIVING
THE DARK

IN 4

THE EUROPEAN MOLE LIVES MOST OF ITS LIFE IN TUNNELS UNDERGROUND. It is active both day and night, using its shovel-like forelimbs to dig through the soil, where it feasts on earthworms and insects that drop into its tunnel. This subterranean lifestyle is shared by many other creatures that shun the light in favour of the dark. Some, like the mole, live undergound in tunnels and burrows. Others choose the hidden worlds of caves and caverns. In the heart of the Sarawak rain forest in Borneo, for instance, bats and cave swiftlets use echolocation to navigate around the deep, dark caves where they roost. There are nocturnal animals, like owls, that sleep by day and use their supersight to hunt at night. And then there are animals that live in permanent darkness in the deep sea: some of these underwater creatures generate their own light sources, which are used in various ways.

BEYOND DAYLIGHT

One of the most noticeable features of nocturnal animals is the size of their eyes. An owl's large, forward-facing eyes take up almost half its skull.

UNLIKE HUMANS, FOR WHOM TOTAL DARKNESS CAN BE BEWILDERING, EVEN FRIGHTENING, FOR MANY ANIMALS IT IS THEIR NATURAL MILIEU. These are the nocturnal animals and they have developed highly specialised senses to enable them to see, hear or smell in the dark. Being part of this night shift has advantages. The darkness acts as a kind of camouflage, enabling predators to approach prey unobserved, while at the same time affording cover for the prey. And being active while others sleep helps to reduce the competition for resources.

Night vision

One of the most noticeable features of nocturnal animals is the size of their eyes. An owl's large, forward-facing eyes take up almost half its skull. The owl cannot move its eyes, but its long, flexible neck enables it to turn its head around and almost upside down to follow its prey. Like many other nocturnal animals, the owl's eyes are specially adapted so they can see in very low light. Most vertebrates have two kinds of light-sensitive cells in their eyes: cones and rods. Cones work in brighter light and register detail and colour, while rods are sensitive to movement and general visual information and are more useful at night. In owls, the retina is mostly composed of rods, with few cones, which means that although they have little colour vision, they can see extraordinarily well at very low light levels, such as by moonlight and even starlight.

Another adaptation for night vision is the tapetum, a mirror-like membrane of reflective cells directly beneath the retina. Light passes through the retina, then bounces off the tapetum to hit the retina a second time, thus maximising the amount of light available to nocturnal eyes. It is this that causes the eyes of a dog or cat to glow in the dark when a light is shone onto them.

During the day, highly light-sensitive eyes would be blinded by bright sunlight, so many nocturnal animals have evolved pupil shapes that restrict the amount of light entering their eyes. The least amount of light passes through slit-like pupils, which close like a barn door. Some animals have vertical slits, others horizontal or diagonal slits. Geckos, for example, have vertical slits that can close up so tightly during the day only a few tiny pinholes are left to let light through.

NIGHT SIGHT Geckos, like this giant leaf-tailed gecko from Madagascar, have the best nocturnal vision of all the lizards. Research has shown that certain geckos can distinguish colours in very low light.

BIG EYES The tarsier has the largest eyes to body size of any living animal. Although its eyes do not move in their sockets, the tarsier has the ability to turn its head through 180°. It catches small prey, such as insects, in almost pitch darkness.

Sound vision

Contrary to a common misconception, bats are not blind. They have functional eyes, but their main way of getting about and finding prey is by echolocation. Bats emit very high-pitched sounds that bounce off objects in the environment. The returning echoes enable them to pinpoint and catch flying insects in complete darkness. The large fruit-eating bats, such as flying foxes, have good night vision and they need some light in order to fly and forage. Their pupils open across almost the entire eye, and the retina is folded so it can capture more light. On cloudy nights, when the moon and stars are obscured, the flying fox will remain at its roost.

Seeing warmth

Pit vipers, such as rattlesnakes, are active at night, when they first track their prey by using smell. The snake's habitat is criss-crossed by rodent trails, and by using its forked tongue to 'taste' the ground, it can work out which rodent trail is in use at any one time. Then, it sits and waits. As the rodent approaches, the snake switches to its heat sense. It has two deep pits, between the eye and nostril on either side of its face, which are sensitive to heat given off by warm-blooded prey. When the target is within range, the snake strikes, injects venom and then pulls back. The venom works slowly and the prey is not killed instantly, but the snake does not lose its kill. It uses its forked tongue again to follow the dying rodent. It can identify the trail of the envenomated mouse from all the other rodent trails, and even tell in which direction it travelled before it succumbed to the venom. It then swallows the prey whole. The snake's heat-sensitive pits are also thought to aid in locating cooler areas in which to rest.

NIGHT-TIME DINERS

LIKE THEIR MYTHICAL NAMESAKES, VAMPIRE BATS HUNT AT NIGHT AND GORGE ON BLOOD. When a victim has been located, the common vampire, which feeds on mammal blood, lands some distance away and crawls on its wings and hind legs. It is remarkably agile on the ground and can run at speeds of up to 8 km/h. Like all vampire bats, it tends to feast on animals that are asleep and its brain is attuned to the regular breathing of sleeping animals. Infrared sensors on its short muzzle help to locate an area on its victim's body where the blood vessels are close to the skin. The bat then sidles up to its chosen patch, and if there is fur or hair in the way, uses its sharp incisors and cheek teeth to snip them away. Using its extremely sharp upper incisors, it makes an 8 mm deep cut and injects saliva into the wound. This saliva contains a glycoprotein called draculin that functions as an anticoagulant, preventing the blood of the bitten victim from clotting. Another substance in the bat's saliva dilates the victim's blood vessels and yet another stops the red blood cells from sticking together. All this ensures that the blood keeps flowing while the bat is drinking.

The vampire bat does not suck blood, but licks it up with a grooved tongue. A 40 g bat might drink up to half its body weight in blood in one session. Under ordinary circumstances this would make the bat too heavy to take off again, but it has the extraordinary ability to digest the blood rapidly as it feeds. The blood plasma (the clear part of the blood) is absorbed by the stomach wall, passed to the kidneys and bladder and expelled as dilute urine. Nevertheless, the bat still has up to 30 per cent more body weight on board when it has finished feeding, and must fling itself into the air in order to become airborne. It returns to the bat roost, where any bat that has failed to feed begs a mouth-to-mouth blood transfusion from one of the others.

Spreading disease

While vampire bats cause little harm to their victims in taking their blood, mammals bitten by them, including humans and domestic animals, are in danger of contracting rabies. Similarly, many bloodsucking insects spread diseases and they, too, are on the wing in the dead of night. Female mosquitoes (but not males) need blood for the development of their eggs. At dusk they set off – often flying continuously for one to four hours and up to 10 km a night – to track down their victims, which they identify from several metres away. Mosquitoes are sensitive to exhaled carbon dioxide in breath and substances in sweat, and they can detect the heat of warm-blooded prey. The female numbs the point of attack with saliva and with its sharp, stylus-like mouthparts pierces the host's skin. The attack itself is usually not felt at all and if this was all that mosquitoes did, they would be no more than an irritation. But mosquitoes carry diseases, such as malaria, dengue fever and yellow fever, which they are responsible for transmitting to 70 million people each year.

Bloodsuckers in the home

Found in temperate climates around the world, bedbugs are about 5–10 mm long, flattened and flightless. They hide away in any dark cracks or crevices during the day, then come out at night to gorge on human blood, attracted by the presence of warmth and carbon dioxide. The bug pierces the skin of its host with two hollow tubes. With one it secretes saliva, which contains an anticoagulant to keep the blood flowing, and with the other it draws blood. Although bedbugs usually feed every five to ten days, they can lie dormant for as long as 18 months. They can be difficult to detect – with only the tell-tale signs of red-blood spots and a foul-smelling odour from their oily secretions giving them away.

The conenose or assassin bug crawls into homes, especially in parts of South America, and uses its powerful beak to suck human blood at night. It also carries a nasty disease known as Chagas Disease. At first this causes local swelling at the point where the bug bit, but the disease can progress over the years, causing heart disease and other chronic symptoms; if left untreated it can be fatal. It is thought that Charles Darwin contracted Chagas Disease in South America, the symptoms of which plagued him for the rest of his life. He described one painful night-time attack in *The Voyage of the Beagle*: 'It is most disgusting to feel soft wingless insects, about an inch long, crawling over one's body. Before sucking they are quite thin but afterwards they become round and bloated with blood.'

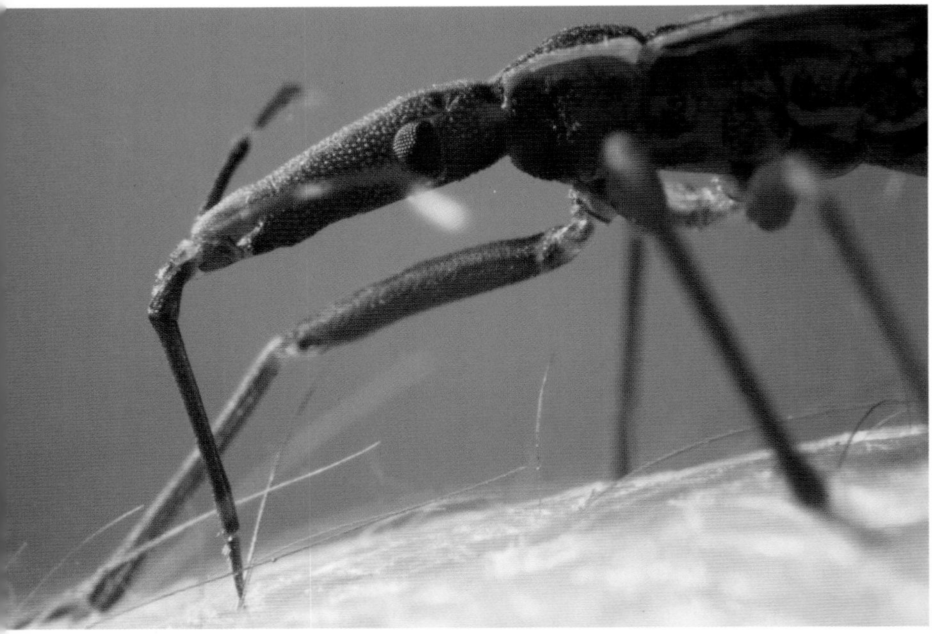

DEADLY KISS The bloodsucking assassin bug carries the parasitic protozoan that causes Chagas Disease, which kills around 50 000 people annually.

FISHING BAT

THE MEXICAN FISHING BAT IS THE LARGEST NORTH AMERICAN MEMBER OF THE GENUS *MYOTIS*. Like other members of the same bat family, it eats insects, but its more usual fare is small fish – such as the mullet caught here – along with marine crustaceans, such as shrimps.

On long, large wings, the fishing bat flies low and slow on night-time patrols over marine lagoons, using its echolocation system to spot disturbances in the still seawater below. It hooks its fish prey by dragging its specially elongated feet and claws across the surface of the water, rather like a fisherman using a gaff. The catch is then deftly transferred from the bat's claws to its mouth and either consumed in flight or carried to a convenient perch.

The Mexican fishing bat lives only on islands in the Sea of Cortez and along the Baja Peninsula, Mexico. It roosts during the day in rocky cracks and crevices, sometimes sharing its space with seabirds, such as least petrels and black petrels. Fishing bats have also been found living under large rocks and tree trunks, and even in empty turtle shells along the shore. This roosting behaviour makes the Mexican fishing bat vulnerable to predation by rats and feral cats and this, coupled with its very limited distribution and specialised diet, means that the species is considered to be endangered.

VITAL STATISTICS

CLASS: Mammalia
ORDER: Chiroptera
SPECIES: *Myotis vivesi*
HABITAT: Marine lagoons
DISTRIBUTION: Sea of Cortez and Baja Peninsula, Mexico
KEY FEATURES: Flies low and slow over water while hunting; hooks prey with hind feet and claws.

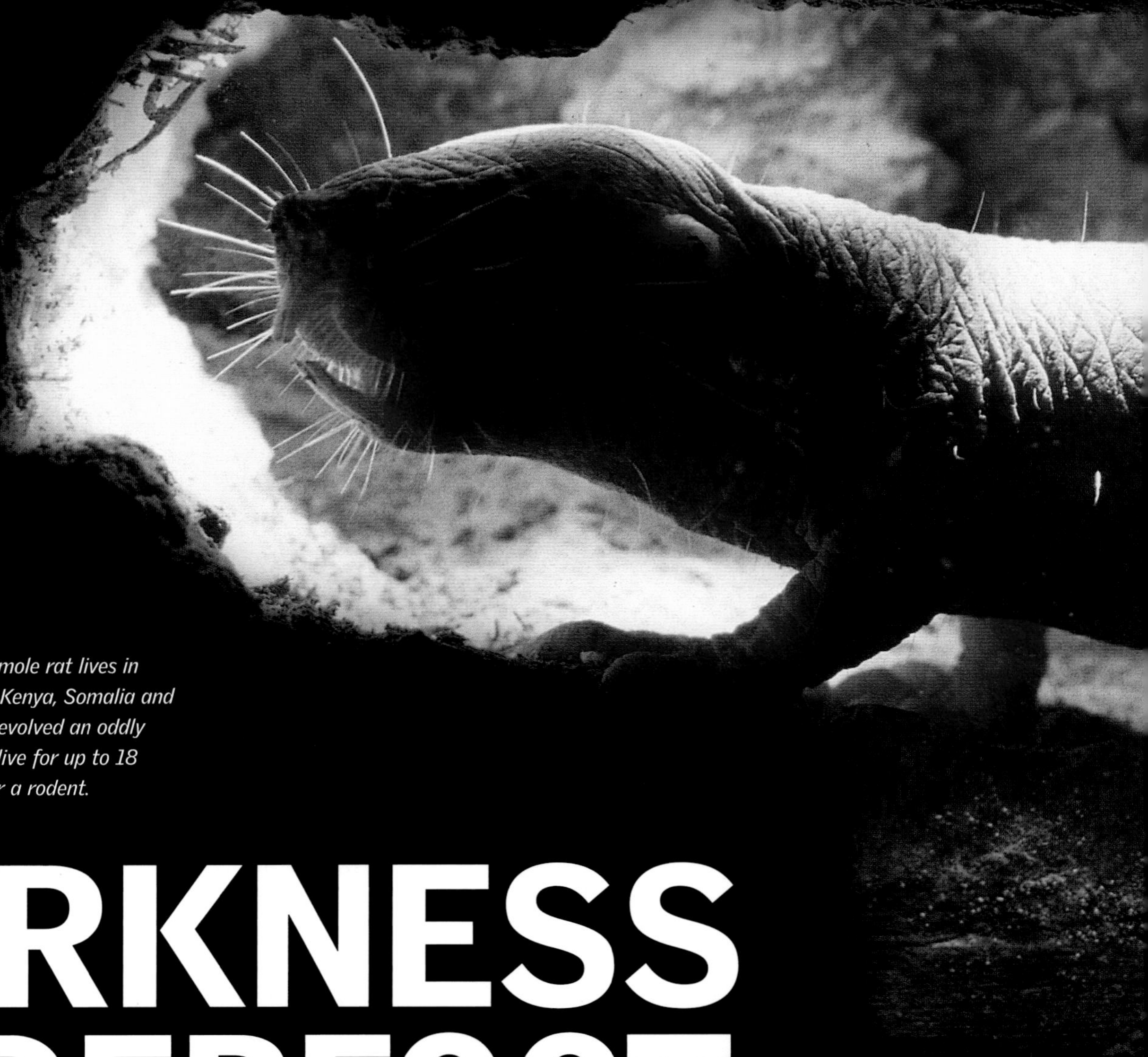

'RINKLY RODENT The naked mole rat lives in nnels under the grasslands of Kenya, Somalia and uthern Ethiopia, where it has evolved an oddly sect-like social system. It can live for up to 18 ears, an unusually long time for a rodent.

DARKNESS UNDERFOOT

N SOME PARTS OF THE WORLD THERE ARE FAR MORE ANIMALS LIVING UNDER THE GROUND THAN ABOVE IT. Perhaps the nost unusual of all are East Africa's naked nole rats. They are unique among mammals in that they ave a lifestyle more akin to that of bees, wasps and ants. They ve in colonies presided over by a queen who selects a maximum f three males with whom she breeds. She rules the roost and revents other females from breeding by bullying them. When ne queen dies, another female takes her place, sometimes after violent struggle with her rivals. The other members of the olony, which can number up to 80 mole rats, have specific roles. 'here is a caste for tunnelling, for example, and another for uarding the tunnel entrances against predators, such as the ... snake.

An individual mole rat measures just 8–10 cm long and resembles a wrinkled, pink-grey sausage. A colony can excavate a network of underground tunnels extending up to 4.8 km. The workers, undistracted by courtship and parenthood, dig their tunnels continually and in an orderly fashion, forming a living conveyor belt. The mole rat at the front of the queue digs with its large, protruding teeth. The next in line sweep the soil behind them until it reaches the mole rat near the tunnel entrance who ejects the soil like a miniature erupting volcano. Researchers have observed a colony excavate a tunnel about 1.6 km long in just three months.

The tunnels lead the mole rats to their food, usually large tubers that are many times bigger than the mole rats themselves. A single tuber can last a colony for up to a year. They eat the soft tissues on the inside but leave the outside, which means the

As they race through the tunnels – as quickly backwards as forwards – whiskers on the face and tail touch the sides of the tunnel and guide the creatures through the labyrinth. Their eyesight is poor and it is thought that their eyes, which are no more than narrow slits, function more as draught detectors. If a predator or rival mole rats should break through a sealed burrow entrance, the sudden air movement is detected immediately and guards dispatched to deal with the intruder.

Oxygen is limited in the tunnels, but naked mole rats have small lungs, a low rate of breathing, and the haemoglobin in their blood has a strong affinity for oxygen. During periods of drought they can lower their metabolic rate by a quarter, but even at the best of times they have a metabolism that is closer to cold-bloodedness than to a warm-blooded mammal. They have no fat under the skin and cannot sweat, so they cannot regulate their body temperature as other mammals do. The temperature in the tunnels must be constant, usually 28–32°C, for the animals to survive. The naked mole rats huddle together at night to reduce heat loss. In the morning, some head for tunnels near the surface that heat up in the Sun. Then, they take the heat they have acquired to their companions in tunnels deeper down.

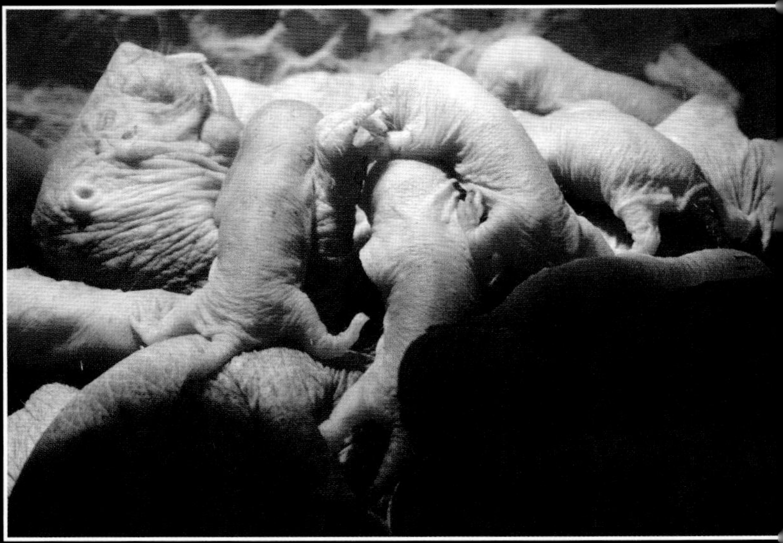

TUNNEL QUEEN The naked mole rat queen suckles her young for a month in a nursery chamber. After this, workers feed the young until they are ready to take solid foods. Litters may contain up to 25 pups.

CAVES

PIT STOP A female Bengal tiger is the temporary occupant of this cave in India. Tigers and other animals, such as bears and raccoons, frequently use caves as safe resting places.

WITH A CONSTANT TEMPERATURE THAT MEANS THEY ARE COOL IN SUMMER AND WARM IN WINTER, caves – as early humans appreciated – have a lot going for them as places to live. In the natural world cave-dwellers fall into two categories: those that nest and roost in caves but venture outside in search of food; and those that spend their entire lives in caves. The latter sometimes depend on the former to keep the food supplies coming in.

The animals that shelter in caves in the most prolific numbers are bats. They roost in caves by day, and forage outside at night. Some caves contain staggering numbers of bats: in Bracken Cave, north of San Antonio, Texas, the colony is 20 million strong. Not only is it the largest bat roost in the world, but also the largest congregation of mammals. The bats are Mexican free-tailed bats, which are medium-sized bats around 9 cm long and one of the most numerous mammals in North America. Each night they stream from the cave, like a long, winding river. During the night, they consume 200 tonnes of flying insects, many of them crop pests, such as the cotton bollworm moth.

Cave-sharing creatures

In the limestone caves on the island of Borneo, bats are joined by cave swiftlets, birds that roost and nest in the caves. Like the bats, cave swiftlets use echolocation based on trains of audible clicks, and therefore can occupy the darkest recesses, sometimes as far as 4 km from the cave entrance. Depending on the species, their nests are made either entirely of saliva, which hardens when exposed to air, or a mixture of saliva and feathers. The

CAVE BIRDS An oilbird and her chicks on their nest in the Aripo Caves, Trinidad. The adult's big eyes give it first-class night vision when it leaves the cave to feed on fruiting trees. The seeds of the fruit are spread widely after passing through the bird's system.

nests, which are built by the male swiftlets during the breeding season, look like a cupped hand and are attached like shelf brackets directly onto the wall high up in the cave. Cave swiftlet nests are considered to be rich in nutrients and local people collect them to make an oriental delicacy – bird's nest soup.

Although the bats and swiftlets nest in the caves, they forage outside. The bats leave at dusk and return at dawn, while the swiftlets take the day shift. At sundown and sunrise, bat hawks wait expectantly outside cave entrances ready to take advantage of the comings and goings of both bats and swiftlets as the shifts change over. Cave racer snakes hang from stalactites in the narrow passageway. They detect the change in air pressure created by the flying bats and swiftlets and snatch their victims as they pass by.

The swiftlets mainly feed on flying ants, termites and mayflies, preferring insect species that swarm periodically in large numbers in order to make the most of their foraging time. When they return to the nest to feed their young, they might have a food ball containing up to 1200 insects. The bats feed on flying insects, too, mainly night-flying moths and mosquitoes. A couple of million bats from a single cave will consume 10 tonnes of insects a night.

All this food creates an enormous amount of waste. Huge mountains of guano accumulate below the bat and swiftlet roosts, and this is food for the many other cave residents, such as

INEDIBLE NESTS White-bellied swiftlets build their nests of mosses and other vegetation in caves in Borneo. The birds also commonly nest in man-made structures, such as under bridges and jetties, and in old, abandoned buildings. Unlike the highly prized edible birds' nests, collectors leave these nests alone.

SULPHUR-LOVING FISH Cueva de Villa Luz – also known as Cueva de las Sardinas – in Tabasco, Mexico, is home to a large population of mollies, fish that thrive in the sulphur-rich water in the cave's spring.

the seething masses of golden cockroaches that cover the guano heaps. There are also fly maggots, millipedes, springtails, worms, mites and moths on the guano heaps. Battalions of cave earwigs make for the highest point that they can find, where they feed on the oils that bats secrete to protect their skin.

Oilbird caves

Another cave-dwelling bird is the oilbird, or guácharo, found in northern parts of South America and on the island of Trinidad. The oilbird's feet are adapted for clinging onto cave ledges where they roost by day, but it more than makes up for its inability to walk with its manoeuvrability in the air. It is able to negotiate the twists and turns of the caverns, tunnels and passageways, and even hover, finding its way in the dark using echolocation. The bird produces a series of clicks, audible to the human ear, and listens for the echoes bouncing off the cave walls and obstacles in its path. Like bats, oilbirds are active at night, a chorus of raucous screams preceding their exodus from the cave. Once outside, the birds use vision rather than echolocation to find food. They forage for the ripening fruit of oil palms and other tropical fruits, such as figs, travelling on average about 40 km each night. It is thought that they are able to locate the fruit by its smell. The birds' common name derives from their fat chicks, which at one time were collected and rendered down for their oil.

Colourless and sightless

Many permanent cave creatures are either white or colourless, and often blind. The cave salamander has no pigments in its skin, but appears pink due to blood vessels close to the skin. The salamander, which has feeble limbs and poorly developed eyes, feeds on aquatic invertebrates, such as cave shrimps, finding them by its acute sense of smell.

One species of fish, the Mexican blind cave tetra, comes in two forms – a normal, eyed version, and a completely blind version. The latter, which have unpigmented skin, are born with eyes, but over time skin grows over their eyes and they degenerate, redundant in the pitch-black world of the cave. The fish finds its way about using its lateral line, which detects pressure changes in the water. Australian caves have a blind cave eel.

Several species of blind invertebrates inhabit caves, the most well known being blind crayfish that live in Kentucky's Mammoth Caves.

SUBTERRANEAN BACTERIA

Colonies of single-cell bacteria hang from the roofs of caverns in the Cueva de Villa Luz, Tabasco, Mexico. The colonies resemble stalactites, but scientists have dubbed them 'snottites' because they have the consistency of runny nasal mucus. The bacteria thrive on hydrogen sulphide bubbling through the water, which means the caves smell of rotten eggs. Snottites are highly acidic, some with the corrosive properties of battery acid, and dissolve the cave walls. Normal cave walls recede at a rate of 1 cm every thousand years, but these caves are being carved out at a rate of 6 cm every thousand years.

CAVE INSECT The cave weta of New Zealand has very long legs and antennae and can jump 2 m in a single leap. Unlike other wetas, it has no sound-producing apparatus and no ears on its legs, so it is deaf.

SIGHTLESS SWIMMER The Georgia blind salamander has no eyes. It lives in aquifers (flooded underground passageways) in Georgia and Florida and shares the water with blind cave crayfish.

DEEP WATER

BELOW THE 'TWILIGHT ZONE', WHERE THE LAST VESTIGES OF SUNLIGHT PENETRATE THE DEEP SEA, the inky darkness of the bathypelagic and abyssopelagic zones shrouds an eerie, mysterious world. These deep zones start at 1000 m and 4000 m, respectively.

The water pressure here is enormous, but all the main groups of marine creatures are represented – bony fish, sharks, molluscs, jellyfish, crustaceans and even mammals in the sperm whales that hunt here.

At these depths, food is scarce and many organisms rely on dead animals drifting down from above, while others feed on each other. Some, with enlarged mouths and stomachs, gorge on creatures bigger than themselves. Whatever their survival strategy, most deep-sea creatures are slow movers. They must conserve energy, so they rely on ambush, surprise and the use of lures to catch food.

FRESHWATER FISH A sculpin perches on a sea plant in Lake Baikal, southern Siberia, the deepest freshwater lake in the world. The sculpin that live in the deep, cold waters of the lake – which contains 20 per cent of all the world's freshwater – are more sluggish than their saltwater relatives. Of the 29 species of sculpin inhabiting the lake, 27 are endemic.

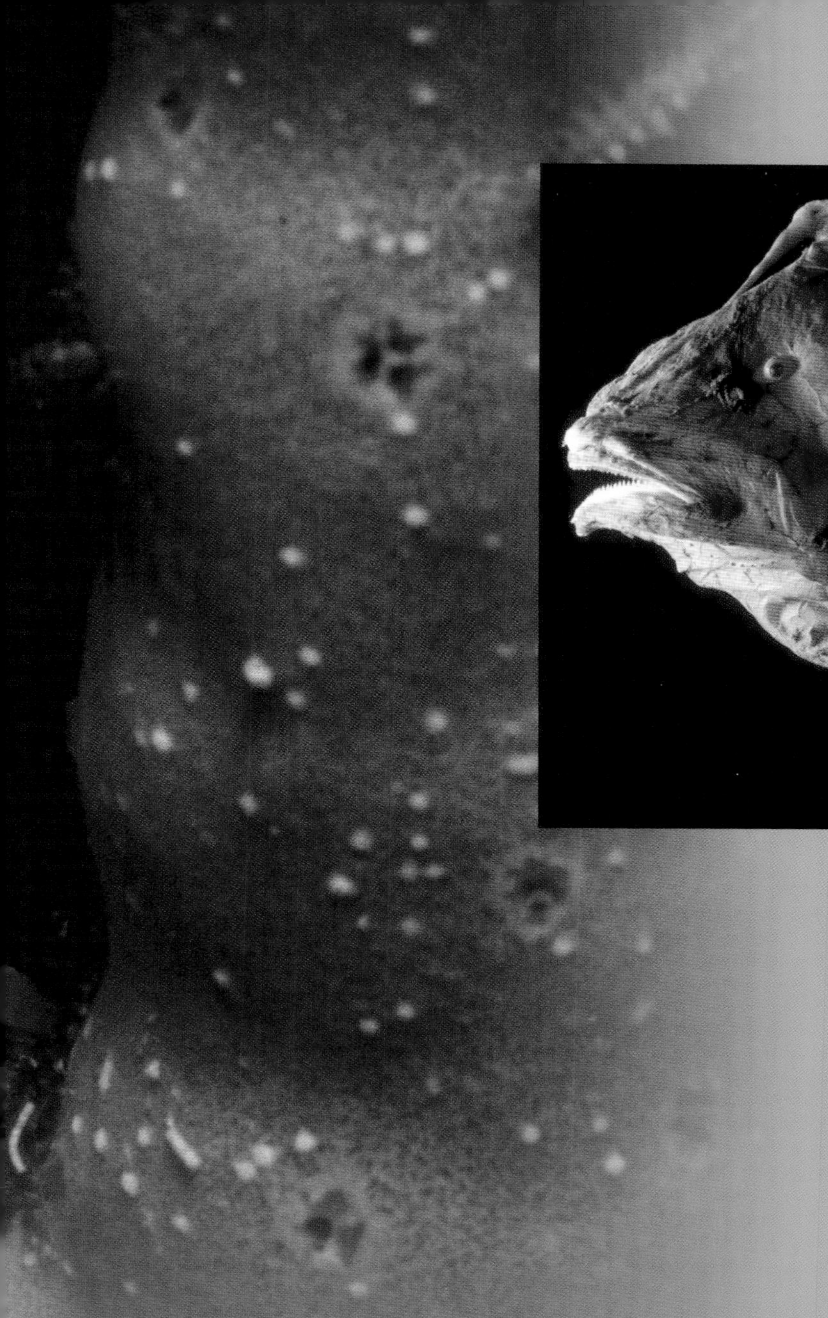

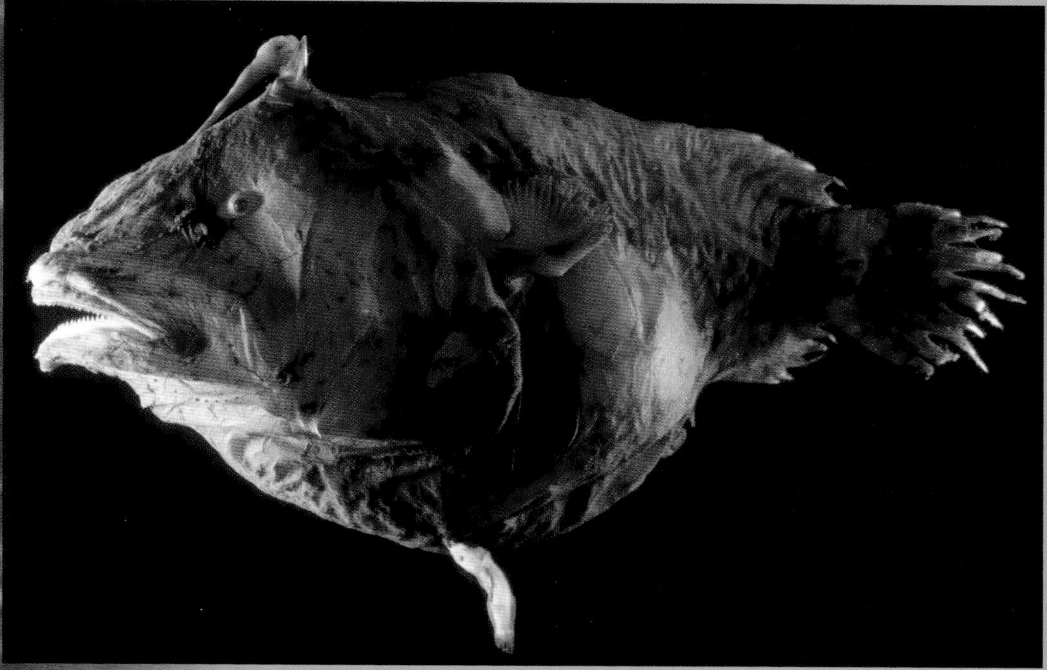

PARASITIC MALE A female deep-sea anglerfish takes her male partner with her wherever she goes, latched on to her underside. After mating, the male, just 73 mm long compared to the female's 770 mm, fuses with the female, obtaining his nourishment from her blood supply.

Abyssal fish and invertebrates

The anglerfish, of which there are many species, has a luminous lure on its forehead that acts like a fishing rod. The anglerfish wriggles its lure to attract other fish or shrimps, which it then catches in its enormous jaws. Teeth in the anglerfish's throat prevent anything from escaping.

Snipe eels are thin, ribbon-like fish 1.2 m long, with a rounded head at the front end and a tail tapering to a thread. Their distinctive bill-like jaws curve away from each other, an adaptation that enables them to catch the deep-sea shrimps on which they feed. The shrimp's antennae fit between the jaws and the shrimp is impaled on the backwards-facing teeth.

With food difficult to find at these depths, many animals must take full advantage of anything that comes their way, even if it is a bit of a mouthful. One of the most bizarre-looking creatures is the gulper eel, which uses its enormous mouth like a net to catch its prey, including animals that are sometimes much bigger than itself. This no problem for the gulper, which has a stomach that can stretch to accommodate large meals.

Deep-sea shrimp-like amphipods and eyeless shrimps, on which many other animals feed, go about in swarms, scavenging on any dead thing they can find. Medusas, relatives of the jellyfish, use their tentacles to grab any particles that rain down from above.

When threatened, the vampire squid inverts its tentacles so the webbing between them hides its body. Spines on the tentacles act as a deterrent to attack. When feeding, the squid drops down on its prey, enveloping it and holding it firmly with the spines.

Basket stars are among a number of echinoderms that live on the seabed, where they use their many-branched arms to collect debris falling from above. Sea pigs, relatives of sea cucumbers, plough through the bottom mud in search of organic matter. Some sea cucumbers have 'wings' with which they can 'fly' above the seabed. Sea spiders, which grow up to 30 cm across, use their long, segmented legs to move along the abyssal mud, sucking out nutrients from soft-bodied invertebrates with their proboscis.

Deep-lake life

Russia's Lake Baikal is the world's oldest and deepest lake. It formed in a rift valley around 30 million years ago and is home to some types of animal normally found in the deep ocean. Two species of golomyanka or Baikal oil fish live at depths of 600–1600 m. They are under such high pressure from the water above, if an angler pulls one to the surface, it disintegrates into a pool of oil and a pile of bones. Sponges grow at depths of 1000 m and are food for the lake's sturgeon. There are also giant worms – one species of flatworm is 40 cm long and eats fish.

MAKING LIGHT IN THE DARKNESS

IN THE DEEPEST, DARKEST PARTS OF THE OCEAN, THE ONLY SOURCE OF LIGHT COMES FROM THE ANIMALS THAT LIVE THERE. Many deep-sea creatures make their own light or have bacteria in their tissues that produce the light for them – a process called bioluminescence. The bioluminescent organisms that live in the depths of the oceans have chemicals in their bodies that, when combined, produce light; unlike other forms of light, it is a cold light.

The main chemical is luciferin; in the presence of the enzyme luciferase and oxygen, it produces light. Most of this is blue–green light, which travels better in water and can be seen by most deep-sea creatures. Bioluminescent light can be continuous or switched on and off. The flashlight fish, for example, has a large light organ below each eye that it can cover up with a flap.

Using light

Bioluminescence can serve several functions. Creatures use it in communication to signal to other animals of their own kind, especially during courtship and mating. Some species of crustacean have coded signals that can be read only by others of the same species. Other uses of light can include a warning to stay away, and it can also act as a form of camouflage. The midshipman fish, for example, has light organs on its belly, reminiscent of the buttons on a naval uniform. Viewed from below, this light display blends in with the dim glow of light from the surface, making the fish less easy to spot.

Deep-sea jellyfish flash their lights as a defence to startle predators, while some medusas cast off light-emitting tentacles. And one species of deep-sea swimming sea cucumber lights up all over its skin when touched. Should its predator press home the attack, the sea cucumber sheds its luminous skin, a strategy that not only enables it to escape, but also illuminates the attacker so that its predators know where it is.

Lured by light

Many deep-sea fish use bioluminescence to capture their prey. The dragon fish, for example, has a long barbel on its chin, which is tipped with a bioluminescent organ. It switches this on and off and waves it back and forth to attract prey close to its mouth, within range of its rows of fang-like teeth. The dragon fish looks an especially ferocious predator, but like many deep-sea fish, it is no more than 15 cm long.

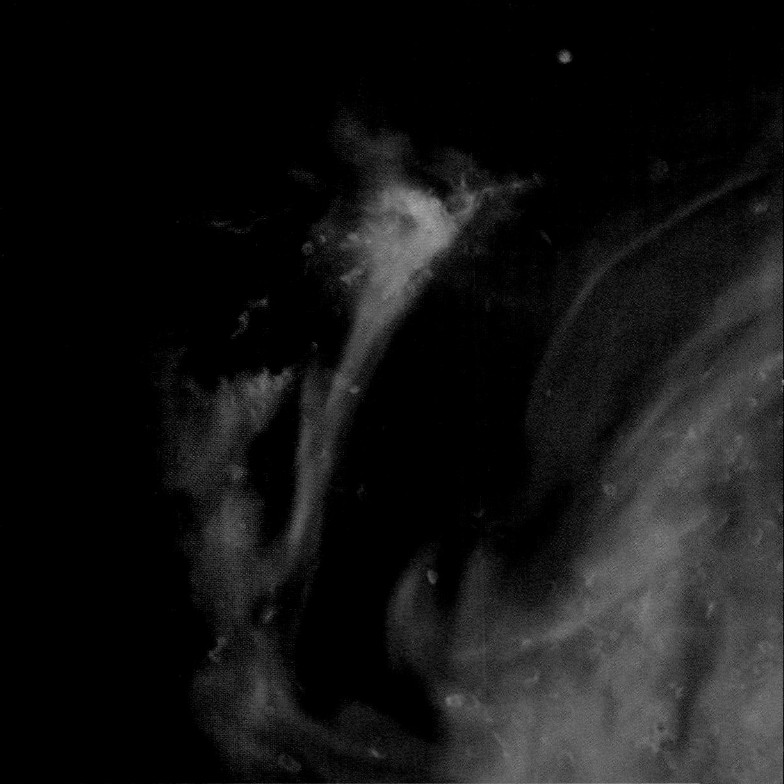

DEEP-SEA LIGHTSHOW The mauve stinger is a bioluminescent jellyfish that flashes when disturbed. In November 2007, an enormous swarm of billions of these jellyfish, covering 25 km^2, killed 100 000 fish on a salmon farm off the coast of Northern Ireland.

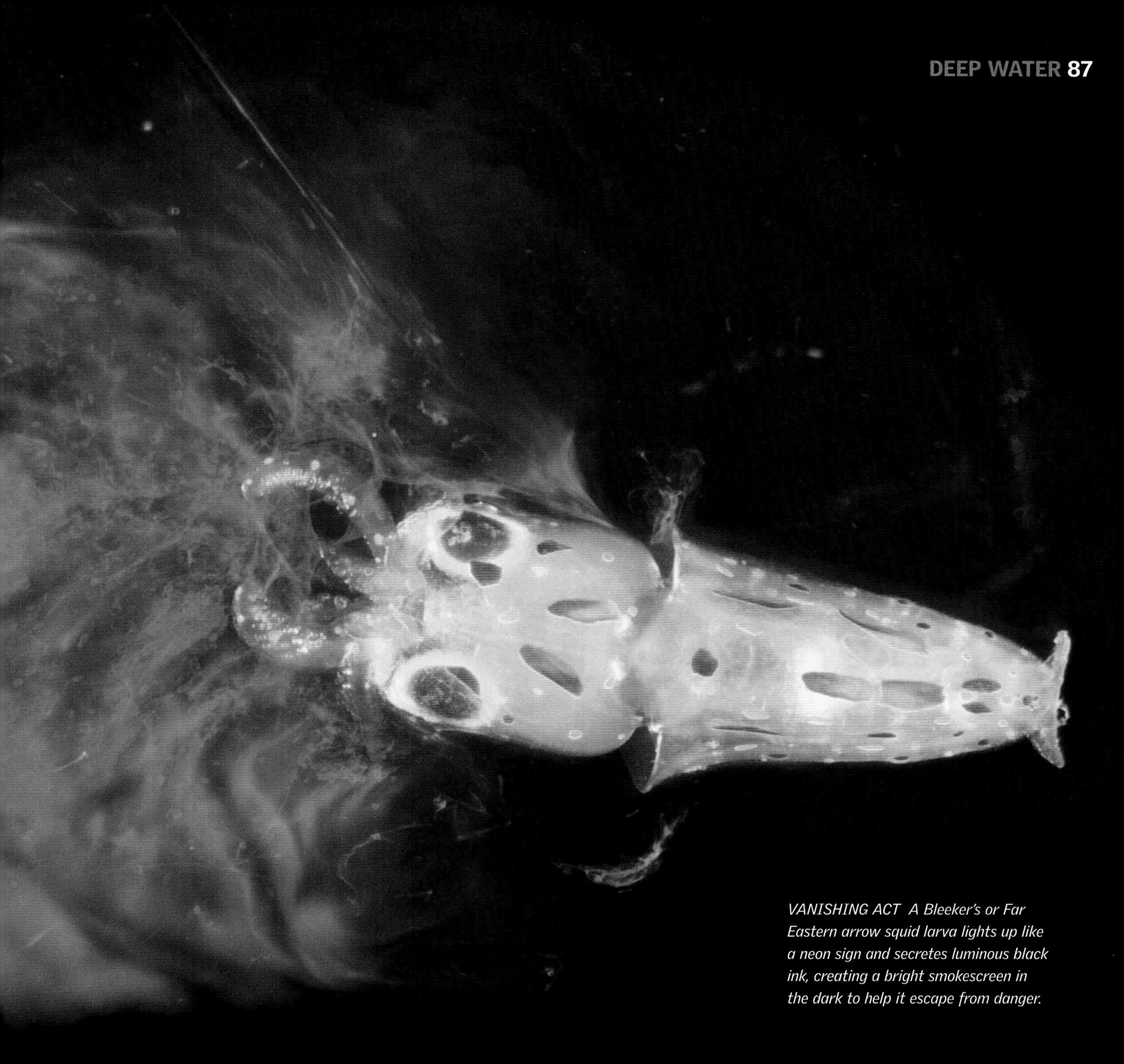

VANISHING ACT A Bleeker's or Far Eastern arrow squid larva lights up like a neon sign and secretes luminous black ink, creating a bright smokescreen in the dark to help it escape from danger.

Another deep-water predator is the 30–60 cm long viperfish, which has a long, dorsal fin spine tipped with a bioluminescent lure. The fish, with a body that is about seven times as long as it is deep, hangs motionless in the water, waving the spine about and switching its light organ on and off. When prey comes within range, the viperfish suddenly darts forwards and slams into it at high speed. The first vertebra, just behind the viperfish's head, acts as a shock absorber, and the fish quickly impales its stunned prey with its very long, fang-like teeth, preventing it from escaping. The viperfish's skull is hinged so it can open its jaws wide enough to swallow larger items and it has a stomach large enough to take them.

The anglerfish has a lure on its head. Rather than fly at prey, it extends its jaw forwards at lightning speed to grab the prey before it can escape. The deep-sea megamouth shark has light organs actually inside its mouth. The shark may be large – up to 5.5 m long – but it is a filter feeder and these light organs serve to attract its deep-sea, shrimp-like prey, which swim right into its open mouth.

The loosejaws, deep-sea fish in the malacosteid family, differ from most other bioluminescent fish in producing red light as well as blue–green light. They can also see red light, while other organisms cannot, which means they can illuminate their prey without drawing attention to themselves.

LAID TO REST

If brittlestars are caught, they can shed their arms in order to get away and then regrow their lost body parts later.

THE DEEP-OCEAN FLOOR IS ESSENTIALLY A GRAVEYARD, THE FINAL RESTING PLACE FOR A MULTITUDE OF SEA CREATURES, from microscopic diatoms to whales. Waiting for the dead to rain down are deep-sea creatures that have mastered the art of scavenging.

Down to a depth of 6000 m or more are the brittlestars, the largest of which can grow to 60 cm across. They are relatively common seabed animals and a carpet of them can cover great swathes of the ocean floor. Each animal consists of a central disc to which are attached five slender arms with rows of tube feet on their underside. Using their flexible arms like limbs, they move by crawling across the seabed, where they feed on detritus that has drifted down from the surface. As a brittlestar settles onto the bottom ooze, its tube feet pass particles to a mouth fringed by 10 jaws. Digestion occurs in the 10 pockets of the stomach. Brittlestars also prey on worms and burrowing crustaceans and molluscs. In the ocean foodchain, brittlestars fall prey to other starfish, such as 10-armed sunstars, but they do have an escape trick. If they are caught, they can shed their arms in order to get away and then regrow their lost body parts later.

Most scavengers on the sea floor rely on their sense of smell to pinpoint carcasses, but some, such as pandalid shrimps, are alerted to the arrival of a new source of food by the infinitesimally small vibrations that a carcass produces when it falls onto the sea floor. The shrimps can pick up this 'micro-seismic-event' from several metres away, relying then on their chemosensory system to home in on the food. They take no more than 20 minutes to find the food source and start feeding. Their activity summons more scavengers, and crabs, rattail fish and huge six-gill and sleeper sharks arrive to claim their share.

STAR WARS A 10-armed sunstar settles to feed on a carpet of five-armed brittlestars. As starfish go, the sunstar is a relatively fast mover. One species, the Pacific sunstar, is able to move across the seabed at 75 cm per minute.

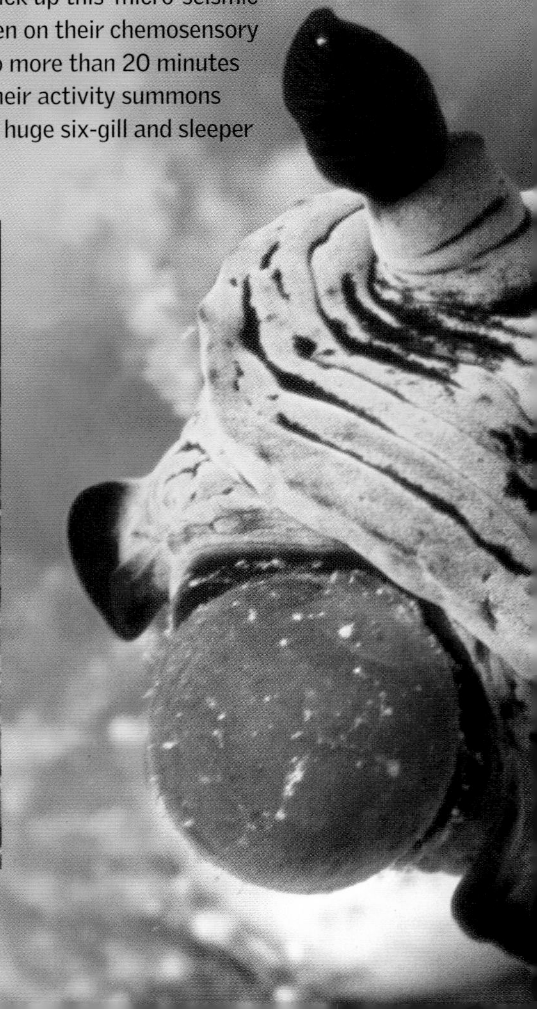

Slimy scavenger

The hagfish is up to 75 cm long and shaped like an eel, but it has no jaws. The mouth is simply a round opening at one end of the fish, surrounded by sensory barbels. The hagfish's skin has no scales and its skeleton is made of cartilage; its eyes are poorly developed. The hagfish also has the distinction of being one of the slimiest animals in the world. Its body is covered with glands that produce copious quantities of a thick, sticky slime, which unlike most other slimes, is reinforced with fibres. Any predator that tries to grab a hagfish has its mouth gummed up with this slime. Fish can smother if their gills get clogged up. The hagfish avoids being smothered by its own slime by tying itself in a knot and passing the knot down its body to wipe the slime away. It feeds on anything, dead or alive; using its tongue to rasp a hole into its victim's body, the hagfish wriggles inside and devours its prey from the inside out.

GRAZING CARNIVORES Nudibranchs are a suborder of sea slugs with different species that live at all depths of the ocean. This one specialises in feeding on tunicates, which it grazes using a tongue-like radula lined with teeth.

MOUNT REFUGE

AIN

5

WILD YAKS LIVE AT ALTITUDES OF UP TO 5400 M ON THE HIGH TREELESS UPLANDS OF THE HIMALAYAS and as far north as Mongolia. They are huge beasts, standing about 2 m at the shoulder – somewhat larger than their domestic relatives – and they survive on a diet of grasses, lichens and other mountain plants. Long shaggy hair keeps them warm, and they secrete a sticky sweat that binds the hair together for extra insulation. They need this protection, for with increasing altitude the climate grows colder and the air thinner. It is a harsh environment, scoured by biting winds and enveloped by subzero temperatures. Yet yaks are far from being the only inhabitants of such regions. Across the world, nature's mountaineers include goats and sheep, rock rabbits, wild asses, alpine plants that grow to gigantic proportions and ice worms that live in glaciers.

GOING UP

THE HIGHEST MOUNTAIN PEAKS AND GLACIERS LOOK LIFELESS, YET A SURPRISING NUMBER OF INSECTS SPECIALISE IN HIGH-ALTITUDE LIVING. In 1982, for example, a Japanese scientist discovered a species of midge on the Yala Glacier, high in the Nepalese Himalayas, which remains active in temperatures as low as –16°C. The adult midge has reduced wings and antennae, so cannot fly; instead, it walks on the surface of the glacier and in small cavities beneath. The insect larvae grow in meltwater drainage channels under the ice, where they feed on bacteria and blue-green algae.

Beetles and rock crawlers

Many more discoveries of mountain-dwelling insects have been made since, including various species of high-altitude beetle and cricket-like insects called grylloblattids, or rock crawlers. At night, the grylloblattids emerge from beneath stones and out of ice

PEAK CROW The alpine or yellow-billed chough is a member of the crow family that lives and breeds in the highest mountain ranges of Europe and Asia. It rarely descends below 1500 m, feeding mainly on insects in summer and berries in winter.

crevices to feed on smaller insects. Often, insects end up on the mountaintops without meaning to – gnats and midges get blown from lower levels in updraughts of warm air, providing a veritable smorgasbord for the grylloblattids and other creatures living there.

In North America, *Nebria* glacier beetles are small black beetles, no bigger than earwigs. Their enzymes function at low temperatures, allowing them to operate at near zero. The disadvantage is that they cannot tolerate warmth – when the Sun comes out the beetles have to dive for cover. Antifreeze chemicals in their blood systems (see page 40) control the way in which ice crystals are formed, allowing the insects to freeze solid in winter, then thaw out again in spring.

Glaciers also have large numbers of ice worms – there can be 2600 of them per square metre of glacier ice. Resembling dark pieces of string, they are related to earthworms but are just 1 cm long. The ice worms shun the light during the day, then emerge on the surface at night to graze on algae and bacteria. Their adaptations to icy conditions make them intolerant of heat: if the temperature rises to 10°C, they die and their bodies liquefy.

SNOWFIELD INSECT Grylloblattids live at freezing temperatures on mountain glaciers and snowfields. They feed on other insects, especially those blown in on updraughts from the valleys below.

THIN AIR

At altitudes of 5000 m and above, the slightest effort leaves most humans gasping for breath. People used to living at or near sea level can acclimatise gradually to high altitudes, but not to conditions on the highest mountains. It is much colder compared to sea level, the atmospheric pressure is lower and there is less oxygen. Mountaineers usually carry oxygen masks and cylinders to reach the tallest peaks. But in high-altitude animals – and to some extent in people born and bred in mountains – the lungs and blood systems are adapted to cope with the thin mountain air.

BAR-HEADED GOOSE Every year, bar-headed geese migrate between mountain lakes in Central Asia and wetland areas in India and Pakistan. This means that they have to fly over the Himalayas twice a year – one bird was spotted at 10 175 m. To help them in the thin air, bar-headed geese have larger wings than geese at sea level.

DEMOISELLE CRANE The demoiselle crane breeds in Central Asia, and one population flies over the Himalayas at a height of 7925 m to spend the winter in southern Asia. Golden eagles prey on the cranes as they are funnelled through the Himalayan mountain passes during the migration.

VICUÑA A relative of the llama and alpaca, the vicuña lives between 4500 m and 5500 m in the Andes of South America. Its red blood cells have high concentrations of haemoglobin, the protein that carries oxygen in the blood to the rest of the body. This adaptation allows vicuñas to extract more oxygen from the thin air.

ANDEAN HILLSTAR Found between 3500 m and 4500 m in the Andes, the hillstar is a high-altitude hummingbird, which has adapted to the thin air by having larger wings than its lowland cousins. It saves energy by perching to feed, rather than hovering like other hummingbirds. The male has a brilliant emerald green throat with a black stripe above a white breast.

ANDEAN MOUNTAIN CAT South America's miniature version of the snow leopard is the size of a domestic cat with a large bushy, striped tail. It lives in the high Andes, and has been seen above the timberline at altitudes of up to 5100 m.

HIMALAYAN MONAL PHEASANT Each year, the Himalayan monal pheasant migrates vertically between its winter habitat at around 2100 m above sea level and its summer home, which reaches altitudes of 4500 m. At the lower altitudes, the pheasant is among open montane forest. Its summer habitat, where it breeds, is above the timberline.

MONGOLIAN SAND PLOVER The Mongolian, or lesser, sand plover spends the winter at sea level, foraging for insects and crustaceans on tidal mud flats around the Indian and south-western Pacific Oceans. In summer, the plover migrates to altitudes of up to 4500 m in the Himalayas and eastern Siberia, where it nests on open ground above the timberline.

A SURE GRIP

THE CLIFF FACE IS VERTICAL WHILE THE LEDGES ARE NO MORE THAN A FEW CENTIMETRES WIDE. Yet wild mountain goats and sheep leap across cracks and crevices and clamber around the crumbling rock as easily as if they were on flat ground. These hardy animals adopted a high-altitude lifestyle because the danger from predators outweighed the risk of falling. The strategy paid off as they became nimble enough to minimise both risks.

SURE-FOOTED LEAPER The North American mountain goat is at home on high narrow ledges that are out of the reach of predators. Both nannies and billies have horns and beards. The billy stands 1 m at the shoulder. Mountain goats feed on moss, lichen, grasses, sedges and low-growing shrubs and conifers.

A loner, but a warm one, the North American mountain goat has two layers of fur consisting of fine, dense under-wool and long, hollow guard hairs.

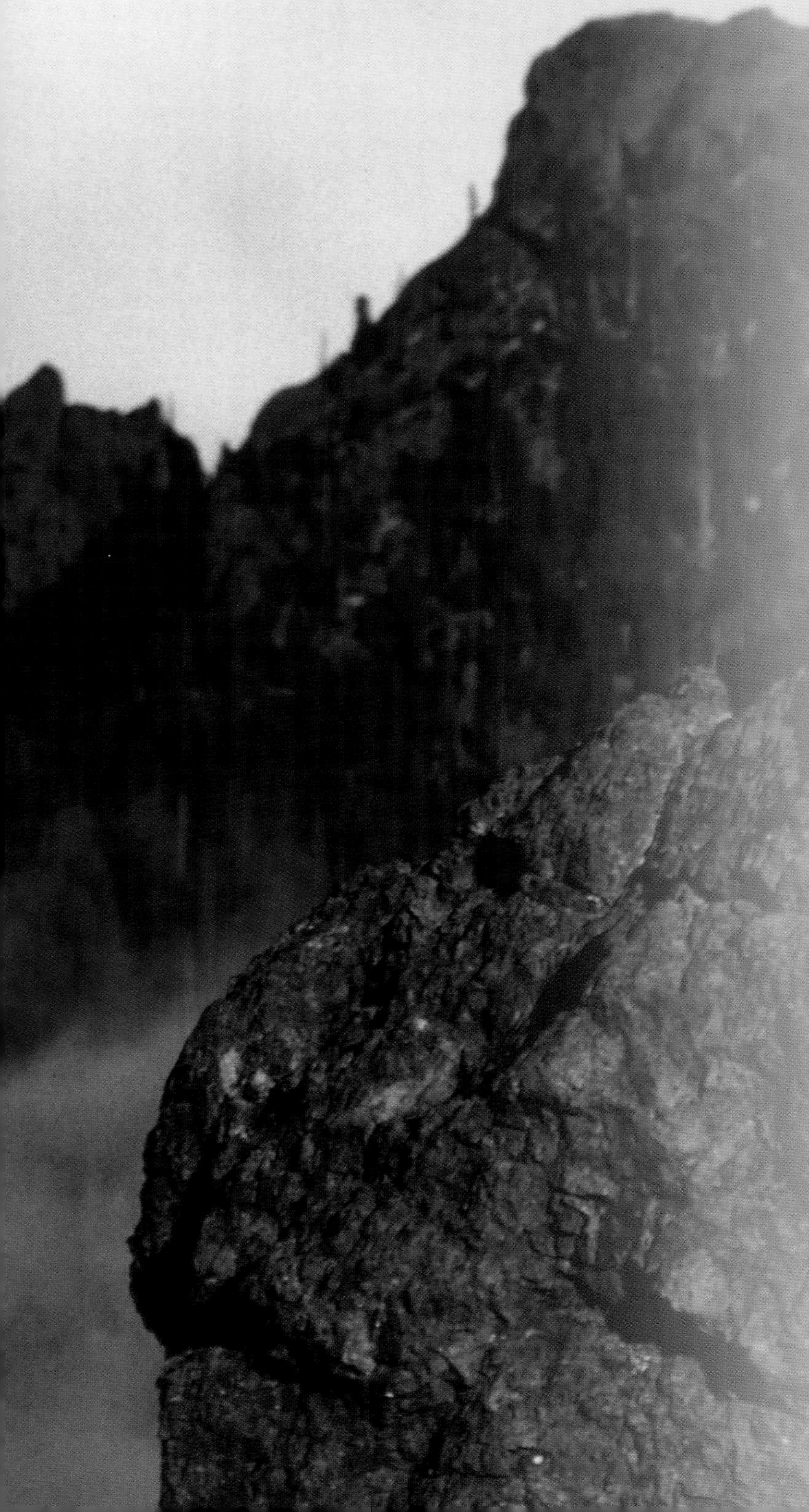

Goat antelopes

Collectively, the world's various goat and sheep species are known as goat antelopes. Within this subfamily, the mountain species that survive the most extreme conditions are the North American (or Rocky) mountain goat and the European chamois.

The mountain goat is a hefty, slow-moving rock climber, which clings to cliffs as it goes to places where no other creature would dare to tread, mainly in the Rockies and Cascade Range, usually above the treeline at altitudes of up to 3000 m. A loner, but a warm one, the mountain goat has two layers of fur consisting of fine, dense underwool and long, hollow guard hairs. The guard hairs form a stiff mane on its neck and rump and 'pantaloons' on its legs. With this double coat, it withstands temperatures that plummet to −46°C and winds of 160 km/h. Its sturdy legs have large cloven hoofs, which can spread apart to give extra grip. The hoofs also have inner pads and dewclaws that help traction on slopes with a pitch of 60 degrees or more and on narrow ledges on near-vertical cliffs.

The females or nannies are exceptionally aggressive in defending food sources from one another. They have horns like the males and do not hesitate to use them. They circle around each other and if things come to blows, one or both of the combatants may receive serious injuries. During the birthing season in spring, the nanny goats come down below the treeline and attack anything that threatens their offspring. Mountain lions, wolves, wolverines, lynx and bears have all been on the wrong end of a female mountain goat's fury. Golden eagles are a particular danger to the young when nannies and their kids clamber back to the upper slopes in summer.

Chamois, ibex and markhor

European chamois are small-bodied and more lightly built than the mountain goats. They are also more gregarious as the females tend to gather into herds, although the males live mainly solitary lives. In summer, they are found above 1800 m in the Alps, the Italian Apennines, the Carpathian and Tatra ranges of Central Europe and in the Caucasus between Europe and Asia. There is also a Pyrenean species of chamois.

In summer, chamois graze on alpine meadows (high-altitude grasslands). In winter, they drop to lower forested levels, but always stay close to the safety of steep cliffs. When a chamois senses danger, it 'sneezes' an alarm call, stamps its feet, then takes off at high speed to the most inaccessible place. It is both nimble and agile, leaping as high as 2 m and across gaps up to 6 m wide. At full tilt, chamois can travel at 50 km/h across slopes and uneven ground.

In Spain, Central Europe and the mountainous regions of southern and Central Asia, the ibex lives on steep, rough terrain at altitudes of up to 4500 m. It spends most of the day on rugged cliffs, but in the early morning and late afternoon it descends to alpine meadows to feed. The males sport massive horns that curve backwards and have ridges on the front, while the females have smaller, slow-growing horns. The males engage in 'playfights', in which they rear up on their hind legs and then

MOUNTAIN WALLABY The black-footed rock-wallaby or warru lives in Western Australia in groups of up to 100 individuals. It feeds at night and rarely drinks, getting all the water its needs from its diet of fruits and herbs.

clash their horns together, but during the rut (mating season), high-ranking male ibex avoid fighting – their horns are potentially lethal weapons and serious tussles can result in injury or death.

The markhor of Afghanistan, Pakistan and northern India is the most primitive mountain goat – the one believed to be closest to the common ancestor of all goat antelopes. It is also the largest member of the subfamily, standing 65–115 cm at the shoulder and weighing up to 110 kg. Both sexes have twisted, corkscrew-shaped horns, the male's growing up to 160 cm long. Markhors are found at altitudes of up to 3500 m, where one of their main predators is the snow leopard.

Mountain sheep

While mountain goats became specialised for life on cliffs, mountain sheep settled for the pastures next to them. Among the sheep, the smallest species is the mouflon of Asia Minor and some of the larger Mediterranean islands, which stands about 70 cm tall at the shoulder. The most impressive-looking mountain sheep are the North American bighorn and the Central Asian argali, found in the Pamir Mountains, the Tibetan Plateau and Outer Mongolia.

Argali rams have enormous forward-curving horns, which can weigh as much as 22 kg, accounting for up to 13 per cent of body mass. The sheep live at altitudes of up to 6100 m, gathering into large single-sex herds, which may be a hundred strong. During the mating season, male and female argali herds meet, and the rams compete vigorously for mating rights. They slam their horns together, the sound of the impact reverberating around the mountains. The Pamir subspecies of argali is also known as the Marco Polo sheep, because it was first described for Europeans by the medieval Venetian traveller.

In North America, the various subspecies of bighorn sheep are related to the snow sheep of Siberia. During the last ice age, a land bridge joined Asia and North America across what is now the Bering Strait, and among the immigrants into North America at this time were the ancestors of the bighorn, which went on to occupy the Rocky Mountains as far south as California. Like argalis, male bighorns have impressive curved horns. Wolves, coyotes, bears and mountain lions are their main predators, and golden eagles take the kids.

Rock hoppers

In Australia, the marsupial equivalents of the mountain goats and sheep are the 16 species of rock-wallaby. Small groups, or colonies, of rock-wallabies live in rugged, rocky terrain, spending most of the day hidden away in caves or under vegetation. They emerge to feed for about three hours on either side of dawn and dusk. Rock-wallabies rarely move far, normally less than 2 km from their daytime refuge, but when they do travel, they make their way across cliffs, through gorges and over boulders with considerable agility. The soles of their feet are heavily textured to grip rocky surfaces by skin friction. The long tail is used for balance while jumping from one rock to the next.

Groups of related rock-wallaby species tend to live in one of three kinds of landscape. Some prefer areas of loose boulders; a second group favours steep cliffs and rocky ledges; a third inhabits isolated rock stacks. The smallest rock-wallabies are the timid monjon and narbalek from the Kimberley region of Western Australia, whose bodies are just 35 cm long. In north-western Queensland, the purple-necked rock-wallaby is unusual in that it secretes a purple pigment in a band around its neck and head – very rare among mammals. The pigment washes off in the rain.

One particular adaptation of rock-wallabies to their harsh environment is the ability of pregnant females to put their developing embryos temporarily on hold when conditions are unfavourable, such as during a drought. Development continues when the rains come and food is available again.

KLIPSPRINGER

THE NIMBLE-FOOTED MOUNTAINEER OF THE DWARF ANTELOPE TRIBE IS THE KLIPSPRINGER – MEANING 'ROCK JUMPER' IN AFRIKAANS, BECAUSE OF THE ANIMAL'S ABILITY TO BOUND ACROSS BARE ROCK, ALMOST AS IF FLYING. It lives in southern and eastern Africa in areas of steep rocky crags and kopjes (rocky islands in the savannah); there are also two isolated populations on rocky massifs in Nigeria and the Central African Republic. Klipspringers are usually seen in pairs that are partners for life, sometimes accompanied by one or two young.

Standing about 50 cm tall at the shoulder, the klipspringer has thick, hollow-shafted hair, which not only protects it from the cold, but also cushions the blow if it crashes into rocks. Its hoofs are peg-like, with a hard outer band and a rubbery centre for better grip on rocky surfaces. Unlike most other antelopes, which have an erect stance when looking out for danger, the klipspringer has an arched back. This allows it to stand with all four hoofs close together on a small ledge. If danger threatens, the male and female stand a few metres apart and duet a whistling alarm call, which tells the predator, 'We've spotted you.'

In most subspecies of klipspringer, only the males have horns, but in one East African subspecies, the females have them, too, and use them in frequent fights to maintain their territories. Territories are worth fighting for. Food is scattered in the mountains, and each pair have an intimate knowledge of all the food sources within their patch; they also know the best places to hide. They have scent glands just in front of their eyes, which they use to scent-mark twigs around their territory. One field biologist counted 840 black, sticky scent marks that a pair had left along the borders of their territory.

VITAL STATISTICS

CLASS: Mammalia
ORDER: Artiodactyla
SPECIES: *Oreotragus oreotragus*
HABITAT: Rocky crags and outcrops
SIZE: Up to 50cm tall at the shoulder
DISTRIBUTION: Southern and eastern Africa
KEY FEATURE: A dwarf antelope that is sure-footed across bare rock.

BIRDS ARE WELL EQUIPPED TO LIVE IN THE MOUNTAINS. They have feathers to keep them warm and wings to take them soaring along ridges, through gorges and over peaks. One of the world's largest flying birds, South America's Andean condor, a vulture, is a mountain bird. Its wingspan of up to 3.1 m enables it to soar over the Andes, covering 200 km a day without ever flapping its wings. It flaps only to take off, relying on warm air currents or thermals to take it higher.

TAKING FLIGHT

Wheeling in great slow circles, the condor is constantly searching for signs of death on the ground below. As a scavenger, it relies on animal carcasses for food, and since death is never far away in the harsh mountain environment, it is rarely short of nourishment. The first birds at a carcass are usually ravens and turkey vultures, species that are also at home in the mountains. The condor, when it joins them, is cautious about where and when it lands in case a predator, such as a fox or mountain lion, is nearby: the condor is a heavy bird, up to 15 kg, and is slow to get off the ground.

Mountain scavengers

The Andean condor's closest living relative is the California condor, which has a longer body but shorter wingspan. Although brought to the edge of extinction by illegal hunting and poisoning, the California condor was saved by the biggest captive breeding project ever undertaken in the USA. The project started in the 1980s and some 150 birds have now been reintroduced successfully into the wild. Another distant relative of the condor was the extinct *Argentavis*, a New World vulture and the largest-known flying bird, which lived about 5 million years ago. With a wingspan of 8 m, it was a real giant, the size of a small aircraft – a single flight feather was 1.5 m long and 20 cm wide.

PEAK RASCAL The kea is intensely inquisitive. At New Zealand ski resorts, it not only feeds on the remains of convenience foods dropped by tourists, but also pulls apart windscreen wipers and other rubber parts of cars. In many ways, it behaves more like a monkey than a bird.

BONE BREAKER *A lammergeier flies with a bone that it will drop onto rocks below to break it into digestible pieces. The colour of the lammergeier's breast feathers is normally white, but in some places males, like this one, have red breasts, which they acquire by rubbing their plumage against rocks containing iron oxide – they do this to attract females.*

In the Old World, the lammergeier, or bearded vulture, is the largest bird in the European Alps, with a wingspan of 2.8 m; the vulture also lives in mountain ranges across other parts of southern Europe, Africa, India and Tibet. Lammergeiers have an unusual diet, more than 70 per cent of it consisting of bones, which they scavenge from carcasses. They carry the bones away to rocky areas, where they drop them on the rocks to break them open. If one bone fails to break, the vulture picks it up and drops it again and again until it does break. The bird then spirals down to eat the small pieces, usually the marrow first, but the lammergeier's gastric juices are so strong it can digest the bone as well as the marrow.

Rock flowers and mountain parrots

A much smaller mountain bird is the wall creeper, which lives in ranges across Europe, including the Alps, and Asia – in China, its name means 'rock flower'. The wall creeper flies like a butterfly, but climbs on vertical rock walls like a mouse, feeding on insects and other invertebrates hiding in cracks and crevices.

In New Zealand, the mountains are home to an unusual species of parrot, the kea (pronounced KAY-a), which eats just about anything from nectar to carrion. A predilection for sheep has earned the kea a bad reputation among the country's farmers. Under cover of darkness, it sneaks up on a sleeping sheep and leaps onto its back. It then uses its long, curved bill to slice through the wool and skin to feast on the fat from its victim's back. The sheep is not killed by the attack, unless it falls accidentally while trying to get away from the kea, but it may succumb later to blood poisoning.

ROCK CLIMBER *A Eurasian wall creeper climbs a rock face in the Swiss Alps. The bird is a long-billed member of the nuthatch family, able to scamper up vertical cliff faces in search of food. It flicks its wings every few seconds revealing crimson wing feathers with white spots.*

CHILL FACTOR

SNOW PACK *Grey wolves are effective hunters even in deep snow. When travelling, they trot one behind the other, stepping in one set of tracks. On ice, they can get cut feet, and flecks of blood are sometimes seen on their trails.*

In winter, the wolves' sprawling, padded feet, with slight webbing between each toe, enable them to clamber through snow. They also have bristle hairs in the paws and blunt claws that allow them to grip slippery surfaces, while blood vessels help to keep the feet from freezing.

PLUNGING TEMPERATURES, WIND CHILL AND NIGHT FROSTS ADD UP TO A PUNISHING CLIMATE AT HIGH ALTITUDES, one that would be lethal for most plants and animals. Yet remote and largely undisturbed mountain areas are home to creatures, such as the grey wolf, that are equipped to cope with these conditions. This is fortunate for the grey wolf, since human expansion has pushed this once widespread animal out of many of the regions where it used to live, and mountainous areas are among the few habitats left to it.

The grey wolf is built for stamina. A pack can trot for many kilometres at a constant 10 km/h and run for short bursts at up to 65 km/h. Each pack is constantly on the move within its territory, scent-marking its boundaries. In winter, the wolves' sprawling, padded feet, with slight webbing between each toe, enable them to clamber through snow. They also have bristle hairs in the paws and blunt claws that allow them to grip slippery surfaces, while blood vessels help to keep the feet from freezing. A thick, double-layer winter coat keeps the rest of the wolf warm, the coarse guard hair repelling water and dirt, and a dense water-resistant inner layer insulating the body. The thick coat is shed in spring.

The grey wolf is a generalist, eating whatever it can find. It needs a minimum of about 1 kg of food a day, on average; when prey is available it can bolt down 10 kg in a single sitting, which means that it can fast for several days when food is scarce. In Europe, packs track and run down deer and wild boar, and intercept small mammals before they can escape down burrows or tunnels. In North America, the wolves' largest prey is the bison, which a big pack will sometimes take on in winter when times are hard. The wolves test a herd by making the bison run. They then look for the weakest individual and attack the targeted animal from all angles, biting at its flanks and neck until it is worn down. Fit bison stand and fight, in which case the wolves as often as not back off. They rarely risk injury – a badly injured wolf is soon a dead wolf.

Mountain digger

One prey that European wolves will not encounter in winter is the alpine marmot of southern and Central Europe, which spends up to nine months of the year in hibernation. The largest member of the squirrel family, the marmot is a terrific digger, able to excavate soil that is as hard as concrete. It digs with its forepaws, removing any stones with its teeth, and shifts the dirt with its hind paws. The den it builds in this way consists of a long tunnel leading to a living chamber lined with moss, lichens and grasses. Several dead-end tunnels are used as lavatories. One family occupies each tunnel, which is enlarged by succeeding generations to make a substantial underground complex.

During the summer, when the marmots are out foraging, at least one of them stands guard, rearing up and looking all around for the slightest hint of danger. If an aerial predator appears, such as a golden eagle, the sentry gives a single whistle and all the marmots disappear immediately into their tunnels. If a land predator approaches, such as a wolf or fox, the guard whistles twice.

From October onwards, the marmots head underground. They block up the entrances to their tunnels with soil and droppings, and then

MOUNTAIN SQUIRRELS Two alpine marmots bask in the Sun in front of the Grossglockner, Austria's highest mountain. Marmots live in family groups of a male and female with their offspring from the previous year.

batten down for the winter, huddling together in their living chambers and shutting down their bodies. The marmot's heart rate drops to five beats per minute and the breathing rate to three breaths per minute. The body temperature drops to the ambient temperature of the chamber – if the temperature comes close to zero, the marmot unconsciously detects this and the body speeds up its metabolism to create heat.

To survive this period of hibernation, the animals need to have fed well during the summer. Any individual that failed to build up enough layers of fat is likely to die of starvation – a fate that usually occurs only among younger, less experienced marmots.

Warm bedding

A smaller mountain inhabitant, the pika or rock rabbit, does not hibernate. This hamster-like mammal, which is related to rabbits and hares, relies on warm bedding to keep out the cold. It is found in mountain regions across Asia, Europe and North America, where it lives in rocky crevices in boulder fields.

In Australia, a small mouse-like marsupial, the mountain pygmy possum, occupies a similar niche, except that it does hibernate. It was thought to be extinct, but was rediscovered in 1966, living in the mountains of New South Wales and Victoria at altitudes of 1400–2000 m. In summer, the pygmy possum puts on fat, gorging on Bogong moths that escape the heat by congregating in the mountains in huge numbers to aestivate – aestivation, the opposite of hibernation, occurs when an animal becomes dormant in summer rather than winter (see page 152). In autumn, the possums roll up into balls, several individuals often huddling together under the snow for warmth, and wait out the winter.

In South America, the chinchilla, a rabbit-sized rodent, lives high in the Andes. It does not hibernate, relying instead on the warmest fur coat imaginable. Each hair follicle has 60 hairs growing from it, and the higher up an animal lives, the denser its coat. Chinchillas live in clans of up to 100 individuals in a complex of burrows which they flee to if danger, such as an Andean mountain cat (see page 95), appears. They are active at night and efficient jumpers, leaping up to 1.5 m into the air.

GELADA

ETHIOPIA'S HIGH GRASSLANDS ARE HOME TO THE GELADA, A SPECIES OF MONKEY RELATED TO THE BABOONS. Unlike its forest and savannah-dwelling cousins, the gelada has opted for a high mountain lifestyle, chiefly at altitudes of between 1400 m and 4400 m in the Semien Mountains of northern Ethiopia.

Geladas live in large mixed-sex groups of up to 600 individuals, which break up during the day into smaller foraging bands, each consisting of a dominant male, his harem of females and their offspring. They feed mainly on grass, helped by having the most developed opposable thumbs of all primates apart from humans. These enable the geladas to tease apart the stems, leaves, flowers and seeds of grass; they also dig out the rhizomes (underground stems). In the evening, the bands reunite and huddle together to keep warm as they sleep on rocky ledges high on vertical cliffs, where they are safe from predators. In the main, geladas do not attack predators, but a new group in the southern Ethiopian Highlands has to cope with jackals, leopards, hyenas and lammergeiers, and it is more aggressive.

Adult males are imposing figures, with long capes of dense hair. Both sexes have an hourglass-shaped pattern of pink skin on their chests; this is usually more prominent in males than females, but when a female is ready to mate, her chest pattern reddens and blisters. The chest pattern seems to relate to the reproductive cycle and is thought to be equivalent to the brightly coloured rumps of baboons, which females 'present' to males to initiate mating. In geladas, this feature is on the chest because they sit on their bottoms all day while feeding, so any sexual display there would be hidden.

VITAL STATISTICS

CLASS: Mammalia
ORDER: Primates
SPECIES: *Theropithecus gelada*
HABITAT: Mountain grasslands
DISTRIBUTION: Ethiopia
KEY FEATURES: Complex social groups with dominant males and harems of females that form large groups at night. Feed on grass.

MOUNTAIN PLANTS

IN BRITAIN, GARDENERS AND GARDEN-LOVERS ARE FAMILIAR WITH RHODODENDRONS, their showy clusters of brightly coloured flowers a welcome sign of spring and summer. In parts of the country, rhododendrons are so common it might be thought that they have always been grown in lowland British gardens. In fact, they are mountain plants, found in the wild in the lower tiers of most of the world's great mountain regions, except in South Africa and South America. They were first brought

to Britain in the 18th century, but it was only in the early 20th century that plant-hunters really started to flood the British market with the numerous different varieties we are familiar with today. Many of them originated on the lower slopes of the Himalayas and other southern Asian mountain ranges.

In the wild, rhododendrons are successful in their high-altitude habitats because they eliminate competition from other plants. They produce a poison called grayanotoxin, which contaminates the ground around them so that nothing else can grow there. People, too, can succumb to the effects of grayanotoxin. In honey made from the nectar and pollen of rhododendrons, especially a species growing in the Black Sea region, it causes hallucinations. In the 9th century AD, Queen Olga of Kiev is said to have presented invading Russians with a gift of Black Sea honey. The story goes that the warrior queen then had her army massacre the invaders while they were in a hallucinatory trance.

Mountains are multistorey habitats, and climbing them can be like moving from the Equator towards the poles, passing through bands of vegetation that correspond to the different climate zones along the way.

Plant layers of Kilimanjaro

Mountains are multistorey habitats, and climbing them can be like moving from the Equator towards the poles, passing through bands of vegetation that correspond to the different climate zones along the way. In the tropics, the lowest levels are forested, first by tropical rain forest, then by temperate deciduous forest, then a little higher still by hardier coniferous forest. Above the treeline is where the true alpine plants grow.

In East Africa, the summit of Tanzania's Mount Kilimanjaro is the highest point on the African continent, 5963 m above sea level, and the slopes below can be divided into several distinct vegetation zones. Ernest Hemingway's short story, *The Snows of Kilimanjaro*, describes the eerie landscape on the dormant volcano's upper slopes and an encounter with a frozen leopard. How the animal got there is a mystery: there are leopards and lions on the lower slopes, but the top of Kilimanjaro is extremely cold, even though it lies close to the Equator.

MYSTICAL VALLEY In Bhutan, Buddhist monks live in this monastery on a 2000 m high granite cliff known as the Tiger's Nest. Each spring, displays of wild rhododendron colour the surrounding mountain slopes.

HIGH GROWTH Giant groundsels growing on Mount Kilimanjaro belong to the same family as daisies and sunflowers. Their trunks can grow to more than 40 cm in diameter and their leaves to more than 50 cm long.

SLOW GROWTH A Haleakala silversword blooms on a cinder desert on the Hawaiian volcano of Haleakala on Maui. The flower stalk is about 2 m high. Thanks to a conservation programme, there are now some 50 000 of these plants growing in the wild.

The ascent of the mountain begins in the hot savannah bushland from which Kilimanjaro rises. Above 1000 m are plantations and farmland, giving way above 2000 m to cloud forest dominated by ferns, tree ferns, podocarps with narrow furling leaves and camphor trees bedecked with mosses and bearded lichens. At this level there are violets, orchids and a species of red and yellow *Impatiens* found nowhere else on Earth.

At 3000 m the trees give way to a distinctive Afro-alpine heath and moorland, where frost forms at night but daytime temperatures soar. Giant heathers have tiny leaves that reduce water loss, like their low-growing European moorland relatives, but Kilimanjaro's heathers are gigantic with thick trunks that grow up to 3 m high. There are also leathery-leaved proteas, red-hot pokers and giant forms of groundsel, sheltering from the scouring winds in damp stream beds. The groundsel grows slowly, no more than 5 cm a year; the tallest, which can be 10 m high, are estimated to be more than 250 years old. The plants have hollow stems to store water and terminal rosettes of up to 120 large leaves. A leaf bud with an equal number of newly forming leaves sits at the centre of each rosette. At night, the fully formed leaves bend over the leaf bud to create a protective 'night bud' to keep the new leaves from freezing. Old leaves are retained on the trunk to help to insulate the plant's water and nutrient transport system. Leaves directly below the leaf rosette decay, providing nutrients for the growing stem. The plants flower at irregular intervals of up to 20 years.

Higher up again on Kilimanjaro, the groundsel is joined by another giant – the giant lobelia, with pineapple-like inflorescences (clusters of flowers on a stem). At night, the lobelia's mature leaves close around the plant's core to protect the young leaf buds from frost. The plant also produces a thick antifreeze solution. A subspecies growing in drier conditions on Kilimanjaro's sister peak, Mount Kenya (Africa's second-highest mountain), has inflorescences that grow up to 3 m tall.

Above 4600 m, the taller plants are no longer able to grow. Most of the limited precipitation at this altitude falls as snow, and although daytime temperatures can reach 35–40°C, at night icy winds bite deep – an equatorial day followed by an arctic night. This is a mountain desert, where only mosses and lichens can survive in the subzero night-time temperatures, along with an occasional hardy survivor, such the yellow daisy-like *Helichrysum newii*, related to the curry plant. This grows near fumaroles (volcanic steam vents) in the summit crater.

Hawaiian speciality

In Hawaii, another volcanic landscape has its own special mountain plants – the silverswords, one species of which grows only at elevations of 2100–3000 m in Haleakala National Park on the island of Maui. Standing out starkly against the Moon-like scenery, the Haleakala silversword is rare and would have become extinct in the 1920s had it not been for a concerted conservation programme. Until then, people used to dig it up to prove that they had climbed the volcano, while goats trampled its seedlings and pigs destroyed its shallow roots.

The Haleakala volcano is dormant and so the silversword is able to grow in the mountain's summit depression, on the rim and on the upper slopes. It is perfectly adapted to a place where the soil is poor – no more than volcanic cinder – and strong winds buffet the mountain slopes, while at night freezing temperatures envelop them. The silversword's narrow, succulent, sword-like leaves are arranged in a single large rosette and covered with silvery hairs to protect them from the cold and conserve water. The rosette is arranged in such a way that it focuses sunlight on new leaves growing from the tip of the plant's stem, raising the temperature there to 20°C.

This basal rosette may grow for 20 years before producing an inflorescence. The flowering stalk can reach a height of 2 m and have 600 compound pink or mauve flower heads, each coated with sticky hairs to prevent crawling insects from damaging it. When flowering is over, the entire plant dies. Because it depends on insects to pollinate it, a number of plants need to be flowering at the same time. If there are not enough, the insects will not be attracted, seeds will not be set and the flowering will be wasted.

Flowers of the Andes

Resembling the silverswords in some ways are the puyas of the South American Andes. These are bromeliads, members of the pineapple family, and one of them, *Puya gigas* (or *Puya raimondii*), is the largest bromeliad in the world. Like the silversword, the puya has a base consisting of sword-shaped leaves that grow for maybe a hundred years or more before the plant sends up a tall, stalked inflorescence. Most puya species have 1–4 m tall flower spikes, but *Puya gigas* is a giant: its leaf base can be more than 2 m wide and 3 m high, while its flower spike may be up to 10 m tall, looking rather like a huge candle in a holder. The inflorescence has upwards of 8000 creamy-white flowers and produces more than 6 million seeds. Having achieved that, the *Puya gigas* then dies.

A mountain hummingbird, the Andean hillstar, pollinates puya flowers. At this altitude, hovering is a great effort, so the bird lands to feed. Each flower contains a flat space, which the hummingbird uses as a landing pad, grabbing hold with its relatively large feet. The hillstar is not alone on the flower. Like airline passengers awaiting their flight, queues of mites wait in turn for the hillstar to arrive. As soon as it pushes into the flower to drink the nectar, the mites on the flower clamber onto its bill while others, which arrived with the hummingbird, disembark. The embarking mites climb up the bill to take a seat amongst the feathers on the bird's head and then get off at the next flower.

Puyas are found mainly at altitudes of 3200–4800 m, where the smaller species are a favourite food of the spectacled bear – so-called because of the white, spectacle-like markings on its face. The bear is particularly fond of the white leaf bases. It pushes over a flower stalk as it starts to grow and eats the base as we would an artichoke. Bears like sugar, and at this time in the plant's life cycle, the sugars that fuel the growth of the inflorescence are concentrated at the base of the stalk.

ROCK SURVIVOR The Pyrenean saxifrage has leathery leaves to conserve water and stems covered with hairs. It grows wherever a crack or crevice can hold soil, sometimes on almost vertical cliff faces.

The region where the puyas grow is called the *páramo*, stretching across parts of Peru, Ecuador, Colombia and Venezuela. It consists mainly of moorland, with small streams trickling through a boggy landscape of tortora grass, blueberries and high-altitude lupins. Other plants include a giant daisy – the 2 m high *frailejón* ('tall grey friar'), with a stem clothed in soft dead leaves and a large rosette of green crowns at the top. The leaves of the *frailejón* have silky hairs, and the two flower stems protruding from each crown bear flowers formed from dozens of florets.

Another surprise is a tree surviving far above the altitudes at which trees usually grow. The wax palm of Colombia looks completely out of place. Some 60 m high, it is one of the world's tallest trees, towering over the surrounding low-growing plants. The wax palm's trunk is remarkably thin, no more than 50–60 cm across at the base and 10 cm at the top. Five branches sprout from the top, each at an angle of 72 degrees from its neighbours in a perfect 360-degree distribution. Bunches of red fruits grow from the branches in such a way that the tree is balanced at the top. Even more surprising are the palm's roots, which penetrate little more than a couple of metres into the soil.

BIG SKY

HIGH ALTITUDE DOES NOT ALWAYS MEAN JAGGED MOUNTAIN PEAKS, KNIFE-EDGED RIDGES AND DIZZY DROPS. In some parts of the world, such as the Tibetan Plateau in Central Asia, an entire region of high plateaus, undulating steppe grasslands and semi-desert spreads out above 4000 m. For the plants and animals living in these places, their existence is a constant battle not only against the cold but also against drought. The crystal clear air contains very little moisture.

ONE FOR ALL Tibetan wild asses or kiang flee as one across the Tibetan Plateau. Almost everything they do, they do together – turning, running, walking, eating and drinking, all in unison.

Wild asses of Tibet

One animal adapted to these harsh conditions is the Tibetan wild ass or kiang. The largest of the wild asses, it has a long, thick brown coat in winter to keep it warm in temperatures that drop to –40°C, and a shorter coat for the three months of summer in the region. This brief summer is the only time of the year when food is plentiful, so the kiang must put on enough fat to help it through the lean times of winter; an animal may gain 40–45 kg, the weight of an Alsatian dog, between August and October. It has tough lips and special ridges in the roof of its mouth to help it to deal with the tough vegetation, which includes low thorny scrub, Tibetan furze and various grasses.

Female kiangs live in tightly knit herds that can vary between 5 and 400 individuals. They travel in lines headed by one of the oldest females. Mature males tag along during the breeding season, herding the females into harems and fighting rivals, but for the rest of the year they are solitary. Pregnant females leave their herds and head for rocky places to hide when they give birth. Foals sometimes fall prey to snow leopards, but the main threat to adults, apart from humans, is the wolf.

HIGH FLIERS

6

A EURASIAN GRIFFON VULTURE LAUNCHES OFF A CLIFF IN THE EXTREMADURA REGION OF WESTERN SPAIN. While most birds remain just a few hundred metres above the ground, there are some, like the griffon vulture, that fly to extraordinary heights. On November 29, 1975, one of its relatives, a Ruppell's griffon vulture, set the world record when it was struck by an airliner at 11 552 m above the Ivory Coast. Other birds that reach extraordinary altitudes include bar-headed geese, which can fly over Mount Everest, the world's highest mountain at 8848 m. Sooty terns spend years at a time in the air between fledging and breeding, wandering far and wide across the oceans. Insects have their own flight adaptations. Some spiders use silken threads to balloon through the air, often covering epic distances.

AIR LIFT

IN FORMATION *Whooper swans tend to fly in family groups and in long V-formations. Those travelling from Iceland to Northern Ireland and Scotland fly over the open sea without putting down to rest.*

WITH A WINGSPAN OF 2.4 M AND A BODY 1.6 M LONG (HALF OF THAT BEING NECK), the whooper swan migrates enormous distances across the northern hemisphere, from breeding grounds in the tundra and taiga to overwintering sites in temperate latitudes. Each spring and autumn these birds fly regularly at high altitudes. Some even join the jet stream, a high-altitude river of wind that whizzes along at 320 km/h or more at between 6100 m and 12 192 m above the planet's surface. In 1967, a flock of whooper swans left Iceland in a hurry to get clear of especially bad weather. They were tracked by radar at various stages in their journey and were found to be flying in the jet stream at an altitude of 8200 m. Here, they picked up a 180 km/h tail wind and made the journey to Northern Ireland in super-quick time.

Over Everest non-stop

The highest high-flying migrants are the bar-headed geese that fly over Mount Everest (see page 94). Making the journey from their breeding sites in Tibet to wetland areas in

India, they too fly in the jet stream, with tail winds enabling them to cover the 1600 km journey in a single day. The geese can power along at 80 km/h on their own, but with a tail wind they can really shift. They cope with the cold because their active bodies are generating heat, which their feathers, especially the downy body feathers, help to retain. Blood vessels in the birds' wings prevent them from icing up.

At altitude, there is only a third of the oxygen found at sea level, but bar-headed geese, like all bird species, are built for efficient uptake of oxygen. Physiological adaptations include air sacs that take inhaled air, store it temporarily, and then send it to the lungs before it is exhaled. The air breathed in, therefore, is circulated through the lungs twice, increasing the opportunity to absorb the oxygen. Bar-headed geese also have special haemoglobin in their red blood cells that has a greater affinity for oxygen, so they absorb more than birds flying at lower altitudes. Migrating songbirds, for example, rarely exceed 600 m and waterfowl stay below 1200 m.

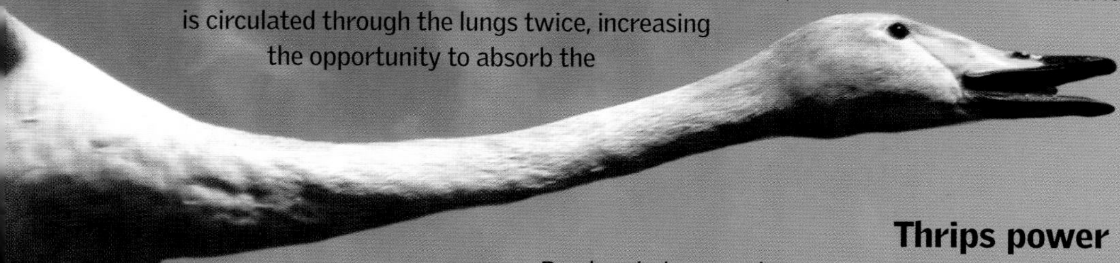

Ballooning spiders

Some organisms reach great heights more by accident than design. These high fliers include tiny insects, spiders, plant pollen and seeds, fungal spores, bacteria and viruses. Together they make up aeroplankton – the aerial equivalent of ocean plankton. Ballooning spiders, for example, use silken threads to keep aloft. The silk contorts with turbulence, changing its aerodynamics and carrying the spider to great heights and over enormous distances. By ballooning, spiders are able to colonise new territories far away from their original home. In the 19th century, when Charles Darwin sailed on HMS *Beagle* in the Pacific Ocean, he saw ballooning spiders 200 km off the South American coast. Spiders were among the first creatures to land on the new volcanic island of Surtsey near Iceland when it pushed up above the surface of the Atlantic Ocean.

The micrometeorological conditions have to be right before a spider undertakes a flight. There needs to be a vertical component to air movement as well as a horizontal one, so spiders tend to fly on sunny days with clear skies, when warm air rises and light winds blow at less than 3 m per second. In order to get airborne, the spider climbs to a launch pad – on the top of a blade of grass, flower head or fence post – and adopts a 'tiptoe' stance. Using its spinnerets, it then produces a silken strand which it lets blow up in the air current while the spider itself is still firmly anchored. When the vertical component of the air produces enough drag to counteract the pull of gravity, the spider lets go and becomes airborne. In theory, by changing the posture of its body and by lengthening or shortening its silken thread, the spider has some control over its flight, but in practice nobody knows whether it exercises such control.

Only small spiders and spiderlings go ballooning. On warm autumn days their silk can be seen strewn across vegetation, when it is known as gossamer, after the Old English term for a warm spell in November known as a 'goose summer'. The Roman philosopher Pliny the Elder (AD 23–79) once described the phenomenon as the day 'it rained wool'.

Thrips power

Measuring no more than 1 mm long, thrips, or thunderflies as they are sometimes known, are weak fliers, but wind and air currents carry them over vast distances and to great heights. When sucked into the rising draught of a thunderstorm, these insects can end up many kilometres high. In the Philippines, one species of thrips pollinates the mahogany tree in an unexpected way. Mahogany flowers open at night, their perfume attracting the thrips. They feed on the pollen but there is more than enough to give the insects a dusting. Before sunrise, the flower falls from the tree taking its tiny passengers with it. The next morning, the thrips are carried by the rising warm air back up to the canopy, where they find another flower and inadvertently pollinate it with the dusting of pollen they acquired the previous day.

GARDENER'S FOE The western flower thrips, a small, slender insect with four feathery wings, is perhaps the most serious pest of floriculture crops in the world. It punctures leaves, stems and flower buds to feed on a plant's sap. The thrips is carried on the wind and warm air currents from one crop to the next.

WINGS

DIFFERENT STROKES To keep airborne, the red admiral butterfly switches between several different flight systems – clapping its wings together, twisting its flapping wing, and creating spin like a tennis ball.

ROWING THROUGH AIR A flock of macaws gathers in the skies over Tambopata National Reserve, Peru. As macaws fly, their wings are constantly changing shape and angle. The action is rather like rowing, but provides lift as well as forward thrust. Macaws travel long distances in search of food.

POWERED FLIGHT – INVOLVING THE FLAPPING OF WINGS, RATHER THAN JUST SOARING OR GLIDING – has evolved four times during the history of life on Earth, probably driven by chasing prey or escaping from predators. About 300 million years ago insects took to the air, the first fliers resembling modern stoneflies, the most primitive group of living insects. Most stonefly species feed, grow and develop as aquatic nymphs and then emerge from the water as winged adults. They skim clumsily over the water on two pairs of membranous wings. Dragonflies are also relatively primitive insects but, unlike the stoneflies, they are expert fliers. They have two pairs of wings with which they can fly rapidly forwards and even hover. Hoverflies go one better. They can hover, fly frontwards, sideways and backwards, and zip off at high speed.

The wings that perform these remarkable aerobatics are extensions of the insect's exoskeleton, strengthened by long veins linked by cross-connections, giving both rigidity and flexibility. Insect wings display remarkable variety. Beetles have membranous forewings but their hind wings have become hard wing covers. Cockroaches and grasshoppers have leathery or parchment-like wings. Bugs have a leathery base to their wings and a membranous distal part. Flies have membranous forewings and their hind wings are modified as miniature gyroscopes. Thrips have two pairs of thin wings fringed with long hairs. Bees and wasps have their forewings linked to their hind wings with hooks, while butterflies and moths have wings covered with scales.

Insect wings are twisted, like helicopter blades, and many have a cross-section like an aerofoil, or aircraft's wing. Mayflies have wings that are hinged in such a way that the insects appear to be 'rowing' in the air. The fore and hind wings of damselflies are the same size and shape and they work independently, giving the insect greater manoeuvrability. These two groups of insects have flight muscles that work directly on the wings. In most other insects, the flight muscles distort the thorax (the middle section of the insect's body bearing the legs and wings) and it is this that moves the wings. In some groups, the wing's downstroke is the result of the deformed thorax going back to its normal shape. These various adaptations mean that insects are the only invertebrates capable of powered flight.

Dinosaur relatives

The second animal group to adopt powered flight was the reptiles. Pterosaurs – the name means 'winged lizard' – took to the air during the time of the dinosaurs about 225 million years ago. They were the first vertebrates to fly. Their wings were leathery membranes of skin and muscle, strengthened by special fibres, which stretched from the body to the tip of a greatly extended fourth finger. In some species the wing attached to the hind limbs as well. The wingspan of some pterosaurs grew to a whopping 12 m, making them the largest vertebrates ever to have flown. They could also be small: in 2008 a fossil of a pterosaur the size of a sparrow was discovered in China. All pterosaurs died out some time before their relatives the non-avian dinosaurs, which became extinct 65.9 million years ago.

Living dinosaurs

The third group to evolve flight was the birds, which first flew around 124 million years ago. Their feather-covered wings have a superstructure of lightweight bone. The bones are similar to those in a human arm: the humerus is short for wing muscle attachment; the radius and ulna support the mid-wing and the hand bones are fused to support the outer wing. The wing has an aerofoil cross-section, which gives lift. The bird can also gain extra lift by moving the flight feathers at the tips of its wings to create slots, an adaptation that is particularly obvious in vultures and eagles. Birds can also twist their wings to make them work more effectively and efficiently – hummingbirds twist their wings in a figure-of-eight pattern.

Youngest fliers

The fourth and final group of fliers are the bats, which appeared 35–55 million years ago and are the only mammals to have evolved powered flight. Bats have an elastic wing membrane supported by the outstretched limbs and tail. The first digit is no more than a small claw for climbing, but the rest of the fingers are greatly elongated across the wing. The wing stroke is similar to a bird's, making bats adept and efficient fliers. During the downstroke the wings are extended fully and they sweep downwards and forwards, giving forward propulsion. During the upstroke, the wrist and elbows twist so the wing partly folds and the leading edge tilts upwards.

PREPARING FOR TAKEOFF
A wandering albatross runs to gather momentum and lift in order to get off the ground. Once airborne, the bird soars around the Southern Ocean, riding the updraughts from waves and barely needing to flap its wings at all.

TAKEOFF AND

FOR BIRDS AS WELL AS THEIR MAN-MADE IMITATORS, AIRCRAFT, THE MOST DIFFICULT PART OF FLYING IS THE TAKEOFF AND LANDING. Speed and lift are inextricably linked, so the flier must have sufficient speed to gain the necessary lift to get off the ground. At takeoff, lift is weak because full speed has not been reached. Similarly, on landing speed is being reduced so lift is weakening. Like aircraft, birds change the size of their wings at takeoff by lowering flaps and opening slots, and they take off into the wind. They flap their wings much faster on takeoff in order to get into the air, which expends far more energy than maintaining flight.

Large soaring birds, such as vultures, eagles and albatrosses, have a harder time at takeoff because they cannot flap their wings fast enough. Vultures and eagles tend to land on cliffs, so when it is time to take off they simply launch themselves over the edge. Albatrosses need a strong wind. Even so, they run, flap and hop in a rather comical way until they finally become airborne and soar with consummate ease and grace. For small birds a jump up is sufficient to get them going. Medium-sized birds simply drop from perches on branches.

During landing the flier must balance the need to slow down without dropping out of the sky. A bird does this by slowing its wing beats, and gravity begins to pull it down. It then twists its wings to create a greater surface area and to increase the angle at landing. Some birds will often flap more on their approach to create more lift momentarily for a soft landing. The tail plays a role, too. It is lowered and spread out to slow the bird down. Nevertheless, some birds, such as albatrosses, often make an undignified landing, ending up with their beak in the dirt. Fast-flying birds, such as peregrines – which can reach speeds of around 180 km/h in a dive, or stoop – have their own landing trick. They aim for a point below their intended landing place, such as a cliff-side nest, and then pull up at the last minute. Their airspeed at landing is virtually nothing, and they touch down, seemingly effortlessly.

Landing on water brings its own challenges. If a bird ditches in the water it runs the risk of becoming waterlogged and drowning. Geese have a curious behaviour known as 'whiffling'. They descend rapidly and then in a series of sideslips, first one way and then the other, they flap into their landing place. Swans put out their feet so they glide and water-ski the last few metres.

Insect techniques

Many insects take off by rapidly extending their legs and jumping into the air. As soon as the legs lose contact with the ground the wings automatically start to flap – a phenomenon known as the 'tarsal reflex'. Flight can also be induced by the wind hitting the antennae. Beetles have an intrinsic problem. Their hind wings have become modified as protective wing covers and have to be held out of the way to ensure the membranous wings are not hindered. The beetle uses its antennae to check the wind speed and direction, and takes off into the wind.

When aloft insects fly in a sea of vortices surrounded by tiny eddies and whirlwinds that they create with their wings. Vortices are the reason a piece of paper drops in an erratic way rather than straight down and are a problem for aircraft, but insects use them to keep flying, especially when hovering.

UPSIDE-DOWN LANDING
Multiflash photography reveals the landing technique of a housefly coming in to land on a ceiling. Its front legs touch down first, then it swings its body up behind them.

Many insects take off by rapidly extending their legs and jumping into the air. As soon as the legs lose contact with the ground the wings automatically start to flap.

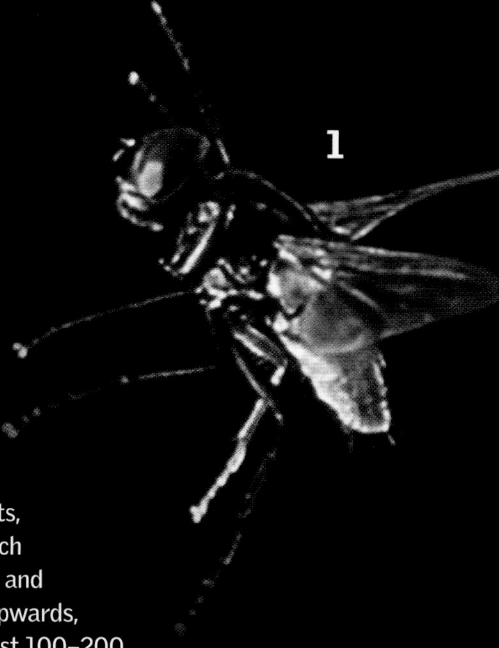

LANDING

Some insects, such as bumblebees, need their wing muscles to be warm before they can take off. If the air temperature is too low, bumblebees can warm the muscles themselves by exercising them, but with the wings uncoupled or the thorax held rigid by other muscles to prevent the wings from moving. When they are warm enough the bee switches its flight muscles back to flying. Theoretically, a bee could keep going for 3200 km on a teaspoon of nectar. The long-distance record holders are desert locusts that fly from Africa across the Atlantic to the Caribbean, a distance of 4500 km.

Landing for insects presents the same set of challenges that birds face. The insect needs to achieve near-zero velocity on its approach in order not to over or undershoot. Beetles tend to land inelegantly, while butterflies execute perfect head-down landings on vertical surfaces, such as treetrunks. For many insects, visual cues on their approach trigger their legs to extend and their body to rotate nose upwards, and they decelerate over just 100–200 milliseconds until they make contact with their landing place. A fly's technique for landing upside down on a ceiling remained a mystery until the introduction of high-speed photography. As the fly comes into land, its two front feet are held above its head. Adhesive pads on the feet are placed on the ceiling first. Then, the fly performs a half loop-the-loop movement and the rest of the legs and body follow. The fly ends up facing the opposite way to which it came.

ALL ABOARD When the harlequin beetle flies, it often carries passengers. Pseudoscorpions travel between decaying fruit trees hitching a ride on its wings. They also mate on the beetle's belly.

WHILE BIRDS, BATS AND INSECTS ARE THE SOLE CHAMPIONS OF POWERED FLIGHT, many other groups of animals have adopted gliding as a means of getting about. Gliding could have been a forerunner of powered flight, and it has advantages of its own. It is an energy-efficient way to get from one tree to another, and so gliders do not need the high-energy foods that many powered fliers must find.

Each glider has developed modifications to a part or parts of its body to form a 'wing'. Flying frogs, such as Wallace's flying frog of Indonesia and the Malabar flying frog of India, have large hands and feet, skin flaps on their arms and legs, and larger areas of webbing between their toes than their non-flying relatives. When their feet are spread out they act like miniature parachutes. The frogs' flying abilities are more

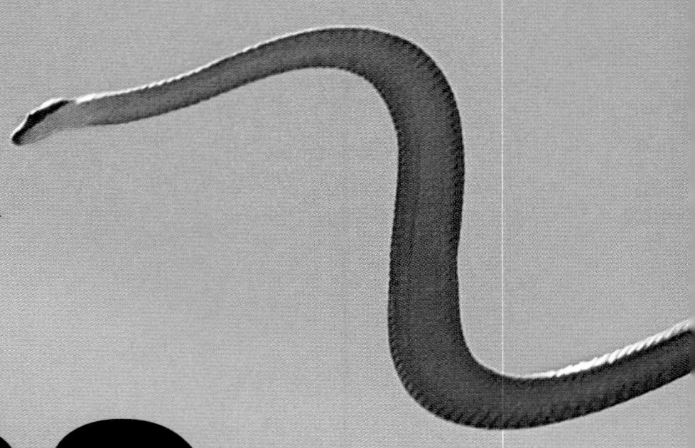

GLIDERS

than simple parachuting. They are true gliders, capable of travelling 15 m or more on flights to a neighbouring tree or the ground, and descending at an angle less than 45° to the horizontal. When the frogs land, oversized toe pads enable them to stick to vertical surfaces, such as treetrunks. Some frogs without these special anatomical features also leap out of trees, but they drop at an angle of more than 45°, so they count as parachutists rather than gliders.

Flying lizards

There are several species of flying lizard, each with slightly different modifications to help it glide. Like the flying frogs, the flying geckos of South-east Asia have flaps along their body – on the neck, limbs, body and flattened tail – and webbing between their toes. When at rest these flaps break up the outline of the gecko, enabling the lizard to disappear against its background. But if a gecko is disturbed, by a predator, for example, the flaps help it to glide to safety and control its fall.

Also from southern Asia are the flying draco lizards, a group of 28 lizard species that have changed very little since the time of the dinosaurs. Flying dracos have modified ribs that can be extended on either side of the body and a large membrane of skin – called the patagium – is stretched between them to form a wing-like extension. The hind feet also have an aerofoil cross-section, and flaps on either side of the neck work as stabilisers. The lizards glide from tree to tree, with flying distances of 50 m recorded, but not when it is raining or windy.

PIRATES OF THE AIR Frigatebirds have the largest wingspan-to-body-weight ratio of any bird, and can stay airborne for more than a week, plucking food from the seas's surface or robbing the catch of other birds (see page 125).

MOUNTAIN GIANT The Andean condor soars majestically on 3.1 m long wings, flapping them at takeoff but rarely in flight. Once in the air the condor can glide for long distances, relying on thermals to stay aloft.

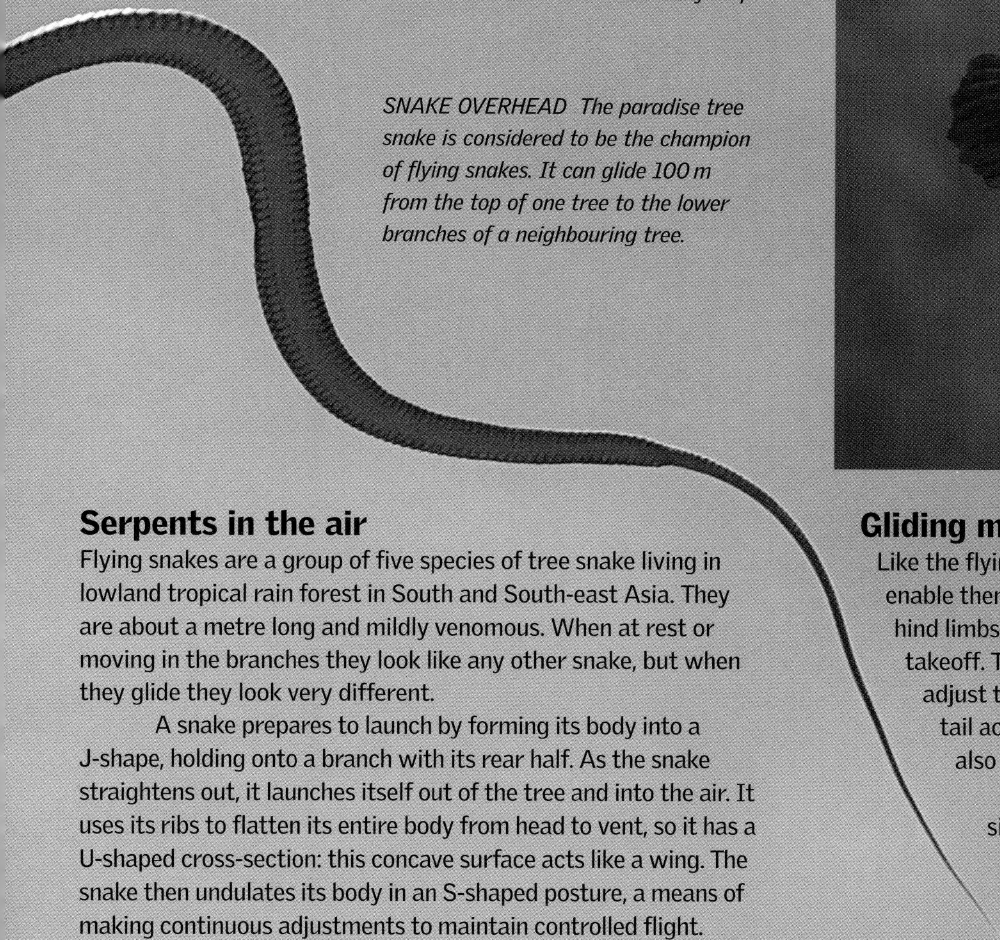

SNAKE OVERHEAD The paradise tree snake is considered to be the champion of flying snakes. It can glide 100 m from the top of one tree to the lower branches of a neighbouring tree.

Serpents in the air

Flying snakes are a group of five species of tree snake living in lowland tropical rain forest in South and South-east Asia. They are about a metre long and mildly venomous. When at rest or moving in the branches they look like any other snake, but when they glide they look very different.

A snake prepares to launch by forming its body into a J-shape, holding onto a branch with its rear half. As the snake straightens out, it launches itself out of the tree and into the air. It uses its ribs to flatten its entire body from head to vent, so it has a U-shaped cross-section: this concave surface acts like a wing. The snake then undulates its body in an S-shaped posture, a means of making continuous adjustments to maintain controlled flight. Flying snakes can turn through 90°, and the tail twists from side to side as balance. They land rather clumsily, but nevertheless this ability to glide enables them to cover long distances quickly.

Fish out of water

There are about 50 species of flying fish that live mainly in tropical and subtropical seas. They all have enlarged pectoral fins, and some have large pelvic fins, too. They use these to glide over the sea's surface to escape fast-swimming predators, such as swordfish, marlin and tuna. When preparing to glide, the flying fish swims just below the surface with its fins pressed against its body. As it leaves the water, the fins are spread. The caudal fin or tail is deeply forked, with the bottom lobe longer than the upper lobe. The fish uses this as a paddle to 'scull' across the surface, gaining speed until the entire body is free of the water and gliding in the air at speeds of up to 60 km/h. A single glide can be up to 50 m, but glides can be extended to hundreds of metres by dipping the tail into the water and sculling some more. Flying fish can also catch the updraught at the leading edge of waves to help them glide even further.

Gliding mammals

Like the flying draco, flying squirrels have a patagium to enable them to glide. This flap of skin between the fore and hind limbs is held loose when not flying but pulled taut at takeoff. The squirrel uses its cartilaginous wrist bones to adjust the tautness of the patagium in order to steer. Its tail acts as a stabiliser, much like the tail on a kite, and also acts as a brake when the squirrel lands.

Australia has gliding possums that have similar skin flaps to flying squirrels. The possums are known as gliders, the largest being the yellow-bellied glider, which weighs around 550 g and can glide up to 150 m. Its smaller relative, the sugar glider, can make 50 m. Before takeoff, gliders tend to weave about and bob backwards and forwards, evaluating the distance and direction of potential landing sites. They then launch themselves into the air using their hind feet, and steer by curving one patagium or the other. The squirrel glider flies at an angle of 37°, while the sugar and mahogany glider's glide path is about 31°. When about 3 m from the landing site, gliders bring their body and hind feet forwards and swoop upwards to land, sometimes with an audible 'plop'. The forefeet make first contact with the treetrunk followed by the hind feet.

Research on sugar gliders has revealed that gliding expends no more energy than walking or climbing about on all fours. Where gliding has an advantage is that it reduces travelling time between foraging sites, which is especially important in the more open Australian forests, enabling the glider to waste less feeding time. Gliding also reduces the time an animal is exposed to predators on the ground, and it enables a glider to make a swift getaway from the likes of goannas, snakes and predatory marsupials, although it is ineffective against owls, one of the glider's main predators.

FACTS

IN 2004, SATELLITE TRACKING by the British Antarctic Survey revealed that a grey-headed albatross from South Georgia circumnavigated the globe, travelling 22 000 km in just 46 days.

THE RED-BREASTED MERGANSER is the world's fastest natural flier in level flight, reaching a speed of 129 km/h. In vertical flight a peregrine has been clocked at 349 km/h in a 45° dive, or stoop.

WITH WINGS JUST 10 cm across, the monarch butterfly migrates 5000 km from the Canadian border to Mexico, travelling at 425 km a day and reaching altitudes of over 3353 m.

FACTS

Up, up and away

Soaring is a form of unpowered flight that looks like gliding but is, in fact, quite different. Soaring animals have very specific meteorological requirements and highly modified bodies. Only large animals can soar, so it is not surprising to find that some of the world's largest birds with the longest wingspans adopt soaring as their preferred means of flying. The *Quetzalcoatlus* – named after the feathered serpent god Quetzalcoatl – was the world's largest pterosaur, an extinct group of flying reptiles. It was probably a soaring reptile, and had probably reached the maximum size for a flying animal.

Vultures and eagles in warmer climes rely on rising columns of hot air or thermals to take them aloft. Eagles in colder regions soar on updraughts of air that are diverted upwards by mountains or ridges. Albatrosses soar on the air currents generated above ocean waves. The result is a considerable saving in energy and the ability to fly enormous distances without ever having to flap their wings.

The wandering albatross is the most accomplished wind-rider of them all, spending much of its life in flight, soaring over the Southern Ocean. It is the largest of the albatrosses with a body length up to 1.35 m and has the greatest wingspan of any flying animal living today, measuring up to 3.7 m from tip to tip. The albatross's wings are long and narrow, stiff and cambered with a thickened and streamlined leading edge to give an aerofoil cross-section. When in the air, tendons provide a shoulder lock so the wing is extended with no muscle effort.

The wandering albatross uses two soaring techniques: 'dynamic soaring' and 'slope soaring'. In the former, the bird repeatedly dives into the still air in the lee of a wave and then 'wheels' back up into the air. In 'slope soaring', the albatross maintains altitude by riding the wind blowing up the face of a wave. The bird travels about 22 m horizontally for every metre dropped vertically – a glide ratio of 22:1. Using these patterns of flying an albatross can travel huge distances for minimum energy consumption. The bird's heart rate in flight is not much higher than the rate when it is sitting on its nest.

The downside of such a dependence on wind and waves is that on calm, wind-free days the albatross must put down on the sea's surface and wait for the wind to pick up again. Takeoff and landing also tends to be a hit-and-miss affair, dependent very much on wind speed.

The wandering albatross can dive no deeper than a metre and it feeds mainly on squid and fish taken at the surface, often scavenging scraps from fishing boats. When foraging, it feeds only in water deeper than 1000 m. With a chick in the nest for about a year, both wandering albatross parents undertake extensive foraging trips. In 1991 scientists from the British Antarctic Survey tracked by satellite a pair of wandering albatross parents breeding on South Georgia. They found that on just three foraging excursions over 17 days the female travelled 13 951 km with an average flight speed of 35 km/h; the male clocked up 9280 km on two trips at a more leisurely 20 km/h, although on occasions it reached 88 km/h.

SOARING SCAVENGER Turkey and black vultures warm up in the morning sun of the Sonoran Desert, North America, while they wait for the thermals (rising warm air) that will take them high into the air to search widely for carrion on the ground.

FLYING LEMUR

AN ARBOREAL ACROBAT THE SIZE OF A LARGE SQUIRREL, THE FLYING LEMUR IS CONSIDERED ONE OF THE MOST ACCOMPLISHED OF GLIDING ANIMALS. The name is misleading: despite its lemur-like face, it is actually a colugo, and it glides rather than flies.

The most distintive feature is a large cape-like membrane of skin – the patagium – that stretches between the fore and hind limbs. This membrane, the largest in any gliding mammal, extends like a blanket from the animal's shoulder to its forepaw, from the tip of its finger to the tip of its toes, and from its hind feet to the tip of its tail. The spaces between its fingers and toes are also webbed. With its arms and legs outstretched, it can glide for up to 100 m between trees. Although graceful in the air, the flying lemur is a clumsy climber, moving in short hops and clinging to the bark of a tree with its needle-shaped claws. It spends its entire life in the trees, sleeping in hollows or hanging upside down from branches during the heat of the day. Its main predator is the rare, powerful Philippine eagle. On the island of Mindanao, flying lemurs make up 90 per cent of the eagle's prey.

VITAL STATISTICS

CLASS: Mammalia
ORDER: Dermoptera
SPECIES: *Cynocephalus volans*
HABITAT: Open areas of rain forest
DISTRIBUTION: Philippines
KEY FEATURE: A large membrane of skin called a patagium enables it to glide long distances from one tree to another.

HIGH-SEAS ROBBERY Great skuas harass a gannet, forcing it to regurgitate the fish it has just caught.

The waiting frigatebirds single out a target, then outrun and hassle the tropicbird until it regurgitates its stomach contents, a behaviour known as kleptoparasitic feeding.

SNATCH SQUAD

SPEED AND AGILITY ARE REQUIRED TO CATCH PREY MID-AIR, and insect-eating birds, bats and predatory flying insects have both. Some wily individuals cheat and steal a meal from under the nose of others. European swifts can fly at speeds of 100 km/h in pursuit of flying insects if they need to. Swifts spend almost their entire life on the wing and their long, scimitar-shaped wings enable them not only to power along but also to glide for relatively long distances. When feeding, they fly with their mouth open, catching prey as small as thrips and as large as hoverflies. A thick fringe of eyelash-like feathers protects the swift's eyes from collisions with flying insects and transparent eye membranes wipe the eyes clean, like windscreen wipers.

Swallows, bats and hawkers

The barn swallow may be slow by comparison to the swift, but it has incredible manoeuvrability, effortlessly making sharp turns to catch insects on the wing. It usually flies about 8 m above open ground or water, catching large flies which make up 70 per cent of its diet. A barn swallow will even swoop down and pluck insects from the water surface. House and sand martins, which may share the sky with swallows and swifts, tend to specialise in catching aphids.

Many of the small insect-eating bats adopt a similar strategy, except they have to do it in the dark, finding flying insects by echolocation. A bat that is feeding is actually going along yelling its head off, but at frequencies that humans cannot hear. When a target is selected, many bats do not emit sounds at a single frequency but in pulses of sounds that sweep down through several frequencies. This gives the bat more accurate information about the type, speed and direction of its target. As the bat gets closer, it increases the number of pulses to obtain even more detailed information. An experiment in Alaska found that little brown bats catching mosquitoes in a barn had a success rate of 92 per cent.

Hawker dragonflies also spend much of their life on the wing. They fly to and fro in their aerial territory, capturing flying insects in a

MID-AIR TAKEAWAY A giant spiketail dragonfly has caught a bee in mid-air and is carrying it back to a convenient perch to eat its meal.

SWALLOWED WHOLE A European bee-eater tosses a captured dragonfly into the air prior to swallowing so that the insect goes down headfirst. Bee-eaters will only catch insects that are on the wing, ignoring flying insects once they land.

'basket' formed by their legs. Hawkers can hover and are capable of rapid acceleration – an Australian dragonfly has been clocked at 58 km/h. Despite the turn of speed and manoeuvrability, dragonflies are themselves chased down by other fast-flying aerial predators, such as hobbies and wagtails.

Darters

Bee-eaters have a different hunting strategy to catch insects. The richly coloured birds watch from a convenient perch, select a target, then fly out to intercept it. Ants, bees and wasps make up most of their prey, with honeybees representing about a third of the food they eat. When they return to their perch, they thwack the bee on the branch to remove the sting and then squeeze it to force out the venom before swallowing.

Darter dragonflies, which can be distinguished from hawkers by their fatter, shorter bodies, perch on a reed, stick, rock or branch and use their impressive eyesight to spot a target, then dart out to catch it. Several species of bat, including the African false vampire bat, also adopt this way of hunting, but instead of actively echolocating for prey, they listen for the sound the prey is making. The false vampire bat specialises in catching beetles on the ground. It perches in low-lying vegetation listening for the sounds of movement, then, in less than five seconds, swoops down to capture its meal. When conditions are not good for hunting on the ground, such as in the rainy season, the bat relies on another technique. It flies along listening for grasshoppers and katydids and plucks them off the vegetation, a process known as 'gleaning'.

Hijackers

Some birds use their flying skills to cause mischief, and acquire a meal in the bargain. Skuas and gulls harass other seabirds mercilessly, forcing them to regurgitate their hard-won meal, but the ace hijackers are frigatebirds and they are a tropicbird's worst nightmare. The tropicbirds leave their cliffside nesting and roosting sites at dawn to feed at sea, plunge-diving for flying fish and squid. By evening, their bag-like crops are full and it is time to return. The waiting frigatebirds single out a target, then outrun and hassle the tropicbird until it regurgitates its stomach contents, a behaviour known as kleptoparasitic feeding. Even so, the frigatebirds are not thought to obtain much of their food this way; it is more of a supplement. At best they acquire about 40 per cent of the food they need by kleptoparasitism.

AERIAL MANOEUVRES

SOME FLYING ANIMALS PERFORM REMARKABLE FEATS OF AEROBATICS. Hummingbirds hover with such precision they appear to be fixed to an invisible perch. The smallest is the diminutive bee hummingbird of Cuba. It is just 5 cm long and weighs little more than a gram, dimensions that make it more akin to a bumblebee than a bird. The bee hummingbird also holds some other remarkable records: its body temperature is 40°C, the highest of all birds; it has the fewest number of feathers; its wings beat 80 times a second during normal flight and up to 200 times a second during courtship. The largest hummingbird is the giant hummingbird of the Andes, which measures up to 22 cm long and weighs up to 20 g; its wings flap at just 8–10 beats per second. Whether fast or slow, all hummingbirds move their wings in the same figure-of-eight cycle, obtaining about 75 per cent lift on the downstroke and 25 per cent on the upstroke. They can do this because of the configuration of their wing bones: the wings have the equivalent of our hand bones, rather than the entire arm, as in other birds. This enables them not only to fly forwards at speed, but also to hover, fly backwards, sideways, upwards and downwards – and even upside-down. The price they pay for this manoeuvrability is that they consume fuel rapidly. Size for size, hummingbirds require 70–80 times the calorie intake of humans to keep flying. Nectar from flowers gives them an instant high-energy food.

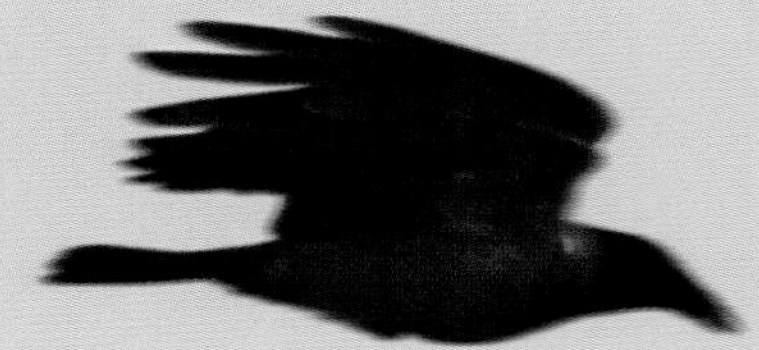

The beautiful sword-billed hummingbird of South America has taken flower-dipping to an extreme. It has a bill (and tongue) far longer than its body, an adaptation that enables it to drink from flowers with long corollas, such as passionflowers, angel's trumpets and fuchsias. The bird's tongue contracts about 13 times a second to suck out the nectar. When at rest, it raises its head so its sword-shaped bill is almost vertical, reducing the strain on its neck. To get round the difficulties of grooming with such a long bill, it grooms itself with its feet.

Hummingbirds supplement their sweet diet with flying insects, which they grab in mid-air. Even this behaviour is not without record-breaking qualities – in order to make use of the energy quickly, they can digest a small fly in just 10 minutes.

Mobbing

Hummingbirds may be small but they are fearless. If a hawk or other dangerous bird should enter their territory they mob it, using their superior aerial manoeuvrability to outwit the predator. It is a behaviour adopted by many small and not so small birds to see off danger. The retaliation often starts with a barrage of alarm calls, and then one or two birds fly aggressively at the predator, diverting its attention away from the nest or roost and harassing it incessantly. After a while, an entire gang of birds might join the fray. Crows are the most frequent mobbers. They will take on a buzzard or eagle much bigger than themselves, while terns, skuas and gulls mob terrestrial predators, such as foxes, actually hitting the intruder with their feet or defecating and vomiting over it with astonishing

MOB RULE Ravens take on a white-tailed eagle in Kuusamo, Finland. Although the ravens are dwarfed by the eagle, by flying at it, diverting its attention and generally harassing it, they ensure that both they and their offspring are safe.

accuracy. Nor is this behaviour confined to fliers. Fur seals will mob a great white shark and meerkats take on venomous snakes. The mobbers do not always have everything their own way, though. There is a report of a great horned owl being mobbed by American crows. It turned and snatched one and made off with it.

Air-to-ground attack

Most bats are expert fliers that catch other flying creatures, but there are a few bat species that take their prey from the ground. The fringe-lipped bat of South and Central America is one such expert. It may use echolocation to find its way about and locate prey, such as insects, but to home in on one item in particular it listens for its calls. The bat's prey is the mud-puddle frog and during the breeding season the male frog calls with a distinctive 'aow' if alone in a pond, but 'aow-chuck-chuck' if there are several males present, sometimes making up to 7000 calls in a single evening. A female frog will react to an 'aow' call, so a solitary frog has a chance, but she prefers an 'aow-chuck-chuck' call as there is more information in the call for her to better assess the suitors.

The problem for the male frogs is that the 'chuck-chuck' part of the call is easily locatable by the fringe-lipped bat, which has ears that are equipped to pick up the low-frequency calls of the frogs. The bat can also distinguish the calls of the mud-puddle frog from other poisonous frogs. When a target is located, the bat swoops down through the rain forest and catches the frog in its mouth, carrying it to a perch to eat. The bat's wings are adapted for weaving between trees. The third digit is longer than the forearm, which reduces drag and increases speed and manoeuvrability. Even more remarkable is the bat's social behaviour. It eavesdrops on its neighbours to find out what they are eating and if one bat successfully finds and eats a new species of frog with a different call, all the fringe-lipped bats in the vicinity soon hear about it and try the same food.

FACTS

MEXICAN FREE-TAILED BATS are among the highest flying bats. They climb regularly to heights of 3000 m or more and when they emerge from their caves in their millions air-traffic controllers have to divert aircraft.

THE BIG BROWN BAT of North and South America is considered to be the world's fastest bat, with a maximum speed of 64 km/h.

NECTAR-FEEDING BATS USE THE ENERGY FROM NECTAR within half an hour of feeding, which allows them to hover like hummingbirds and feed all night.

FACTS

MIDNIGHT FEAST A fringe-lipped bat used echolocation to snatch this lizard from the rain-forest floor in Panama.

FORMATION FLIGHT

LARGE FLOCKS OF BIRDS, SUCH AS STARLINGS AND WADERS, WHEEL ACROSS THE SKY LIKE A SINGLE, fluid organism, each and every bird in the flock seeming to change direction simultaneously. It is one of nature's great spectacles, but why and how do they do it? One reason why is that there is safety in numbers. Many eyes spot a predator, even though individuals might have their head down feeding, snoozing or looking in the opposite direction. And once a predator is confronted with a huge flock in motion, it is likely to be confused. It is no longer confronting a single target, and it could be dangerous to fly into a flailing mass of wings and moving bodies.

The birds bunch together tightly. There is no one leader, for as the birds change direction different birds emerge at the front. In fact, any bird can initiate a change of direction, but only if it banks into the flock rather than away from it. Any bird that turns out of the flock is in danger of being isolated, and predators go for the stragglers. The movement of the initiator then propagates rapidly through the flock. The first birds take 67 milliseconds to react and turn, but further down the line the birds see the wave manoeuvre approaching them and, being prepared, they take just 15 milliseconds to make the turn, which is three times their normal visual reaction time. It is like a high-stepping chorus line, where the dancers are able to anticipate when it is their turn to kick by watching the manoeuvre travel down the line.

This lightning reaction accounts for the apparent random movement of flocks, as birds in different parts of the flock initiate the 'chorus line'. The birds swirl this way and that until a common direction is established, such as setting off for a food source or settling down on the roost for the night. Huge flocks of starlings do this each evening. Small groups arrive from foraging in the surrounding countryside, and eventually coalesce into a huge, dense swarm that appears to move around the sky in an arbitrary way. It is as if the birds are unsure whether to settle or not. Eventually,

HOME TO ROOST A murmuration of starlings prior to settling for the night on the Somerset Levels in the south-west of England. Roosts in this part of the world can number millions of birds.

Eventually, one bird makes the decision to fly down to the roost site and like a salvo of rockets the rest follow, dropping down into the vegetation where they stay until morning.

one bird makes the decision to fly down to the roost site and like a salvo of rockets the rest follow, dropping down into the vegetation where they stay there until morning.

Flocking is also a reassurance that an individual is on the correct migration route or at the right roost or feeding area. It can also be an information centre. In the great seabird colonies that occupy sea cliffs, millions of birds are constantly watching the comings and goings of small foraging flocks. They note especially the direction from which the birds return and whether they are heavily laden or running empty. They then head off towards the fishing grounds of the successful birds.

Strength in numbers

Swans and geese on migration tend to travel in groups and in a V-formation. They do this to reduce energy expenditure. There are several aerodynamic benefits. Each bird takes advantage of the wingtip vortices created by the bird in front. These vortices have a downdraught that is of no use, but there is also an updraught. As long as the bird is behind and a little above the bird in front, it can take advantage of this updraught, which reduces drag, so the bird's angle of flight needs be less. This in turn increases lift, so the bird does not have to flap its wings so hard to move forwards. There are also greater opportunities to glide, albeit momentarily, so each bird uses less energy.

A monitoring experiment was conducted in France with white pelicans who had been trained to follow aircraft and boats for a film. It was found that birds flying in formation had heart rates significantly slower than birds flying alone. It was estimated that a small flock of 25 birds flying in formation could fly 70 per cent further than a solo bird using equivalent energy.

The leading bird in a formation works the hardest, as it is flying through undisturbed air. Nevertheless, the flapping of the two birds that flank it reduces some of the downdraught and therefore some of the drag. After a while a tired leader drops back and another bird takes over. Those at the end of the line do not have the benefit of birds behind so they work second hardest. The best place is in the middle of the line, where a bird gains the benefit of the updraught of the birds both in front and behind.

CLOSE FORMATION A siege or sedge of common crane flies in formation, each bird benefiting from the air movements of the birds in front and behind.

ENDURANCE TEST

AT FLEDGING TIME, EUROPEAN SWIFTS MUST SWITCH INSTANTLY FROM A SEDENTARY LIFE IN THE COMFORT OF THEIR NEST, to a very active life on the wing, so they must prepare for the big day. The 40 meals a day brought to the chicks by their parents mean they put on weight, growing heavier even than adults. About a week before it is time for them to leave the nest, they lose weight, using up the fat stores that had been an insurance against poor foraging. They also lose a little weight by drying out their feathers. Once they have slimmed down, they leave the nest for their first and longest flight. They fall at first, but once they are carried on the breeze, they start to fly and they do not stop flying for about four years. They feed, drink, bathe, preen, sleep and even mate on the wing.

Life on the edge

For barnacle goose youngsters, the first step over the edge comes at an even earlier age. These geese nest on inaccessible cliff tops and ledges, safe from Arctic foxes and other predators, but there is little food up there. Goslings are precocious birds and feed for themselves from the moment they hatch, so there is nothing for it but to leap over the edge into the unknown. With considerable encouragement from mother, the tiny balls of fluff bravely leap out into space. Unable to fly, the three-day old chicks bounce down the cliff face and land in a heap at the bottom. Of those that survive the impact of the fall, around a quarter will fall prey to Arctic foxes and gulls.

The fledglings of some seabirds, such as little auks, also make early flights, even before they have learned to fly. The stocky little auk parents nest on steep slopes and rocky cliffs and at first both feed their offspring. By the time the chick is fledging, only the male brings food, the female having already left for the open sea. The day comes

Unable to fly, the three-day old barnacle goose chicks bounce off the cliff face and land in a heap at the bottom.

MAIDEN FLIGHT A vermilion flycatcher fledgling in Texas tests its wings prior to taking its first flight.

when the chick must go to sea, too. Although hardly able to fly, it 'glides' down to the sea escorted by its male parent. Some youngsters drop short and crash on the rocks or the beach where glaucous gulls, Arctic foxes and even polar bears are waiting. The survivors swim, accompanied by the male, many miles out to sea where they are safer from the predators.

The ducklings of wood ducks, goldeneye and shelduck also have to make an early start in life. Their nest is often in a hole in the trunk of a tree, and not long after hatching the female parent stands at the base of the tree and calls them repeatedly. One by one they scramble to the edge of the entrance and leap. Their light bodyweight and downy feathers help prevent serious injury.

Life on the ocean waves

For some birds, their troubles begin when they reach the sea. On the remote French Frigate Shoals to the north-west of the Hawaiian archipelago, large numbers of Laysan and black-footed albatrosses nest undisturbed. When the time comes to practise flying, the fledglings wait for a stiff breeze and hold out their wings and begin to flap. They do this for a couple of weeks until they become bolder and leave the ground for a very short hop, and then become bolder still and make a practice flight. Some land on the beach, but a few are blown off course and ditch in the sea. They sit there, bobbing in the waves when suddenly the huge jaws of a tiger shark come into view. The sharks appear in the lagoons and shallow coastal waters every July, some days before the birds are due to fledge. It is as if they know there is easy food to be had, and head towards the low islands from all parts of the archipelago. The action generally takes place a couple of hours after sunrise. During the first few days of fledging the sharks are less successful at catching their prey, as the lightweight chicks bob about like corks. After a while, though, the tiger sharks

FLIGHT PRACTICE A pair of juvenile Harris hawks hone their flying skills in a mesquite tree. After learning to fly and hunt, the hawks still remain with their parents to help train the next brood.

SHARK ATTACK A tiger shark moves in on a fledgling albatross that has ditched in the sea at French Frigate Shoals, Hawaii. Often, the shark's bow wave will push the fledgling away and as long as the young bird can struggle back into the air, it escapes with no more than a nasty shock.

perfect their tactics. Instead of pushing up to the surface they rush across it and grab the birds, dragging them below where they drown. Any that get away are sure to ditch again a few metres up wind, and the shark is ready for them. One in 10 albatross fledglings fall prey to tiger sharks.

Wing flapping

For most fledglings, life is rather less stressful. They sit in the nest frequently exercising their flight muscles ready for their first take-off. They may not fly far and often as not end up on the ground. This is the time when people pick them up in the erroneous belief that they have been abandoned. In fact, most times the mother bird is nearby encouraging her offspring to fly, and the young bird will persevere, clumsily making its way back up through the vegetation to a higher perch from where it can get a better lift-off. So fledgling birds should be left alone – especially crow fledglings. A jogger in a London park was running past a crow's nest where fledglings were starting to leave the nest when the parent birds attacked him viciously, leaving him with a blood-spattered T-shirt in a scene reminiscent of Alfred Hitchcock's film *The Birds*.

Cheeky jay

Very occasionally, fledgling birds do the strangest things. In the early summer of 1987, on the campus of the University of South Florida, a fledgling blue jay appeared in a nest belonging to a pair of fish crows and their chicks. When the adult crows first arrived with food they ignored the young interloper, but after a while it struck lucky. When the female bird returned with food she fed her own chicks and passed some food to the male who duly helped her feed the youngsters, including the blue jay. This went on for 12 days, after which the blue jay flew away. At no time did the crows show any aggression towards the young jay. Generally, fish crows raid blue jay nests and will prey on their eggs and young, but they appear to have an inhibition against eating small birds in their own nest – perhaps lest they eat their own offspring. The blue jay, probably unknowingly, exploited this loophole in the fish crows' behaviour and obtained free hospitality. It is thought the blue jay clambered into the crows' nest after fledging from its own nest nearby.

SOOTY TERN

FOR UP TO NINE YEARS THE SOOTY TERN REMAINS AIRBORNE, NOT ONCE TOUCHING DOWN ON DRY LAND UNTIL IT IS READY TO BREED. As soon as a fledgling has left the nest, it wanders far and wide across the oceans, feeding and sleeping on the wing. It often feeds alongside large predatory fish that push smaller fish and squid close to the surface, where the tern can pick them off. The birds have poor oil glands, so if they alight on the water for too long they become waterlogged.

Sooty terns are found throughout the tropics and are sometimes known as 'wideawakes' due to their noisy calling habits. They nest in places undisturbed by people and return unerringly to the same spot each year. The nest is no more than a scrape in the sand, so eggs and chicks are exposed to high temperatures in the tropical sun. Eggs are incubated for 30 days, an unusually long time, with individual shifts lasting around five days, but when the temperature soars they can be abandoned temporarily while the birds drink seawater. The parents shade the chicks and feed them every 16 hours with regurgitated fish. Fledging occurs after six weeks, but the parents continue to feed their chicks for several weeks afterwards. But sometimes, when fishing is poor, birds will abandon their nests. In some years on Ascension Island, in the South Atlantic, thousands of eggs and chicks lay abandoned in Mars Bay. Other threats come from predation by domestic dogs and introduced rats. Sooty terns that do survive the trials of life on land and at sea can live for up to 35 years.

VITAL STATISTICS

CLASS: Aves
ORDER: Charadriiformes
SPECIES: *Onychoprion fuscatus*
HABITAT: Open ocean
DISTRIBUTION: Tropics worldwide
KEY FEATURES: Spends most of its life on the wing and does not dive for food like other terns. It has a remarkable homing ability.

AVOIDING EXTREMES

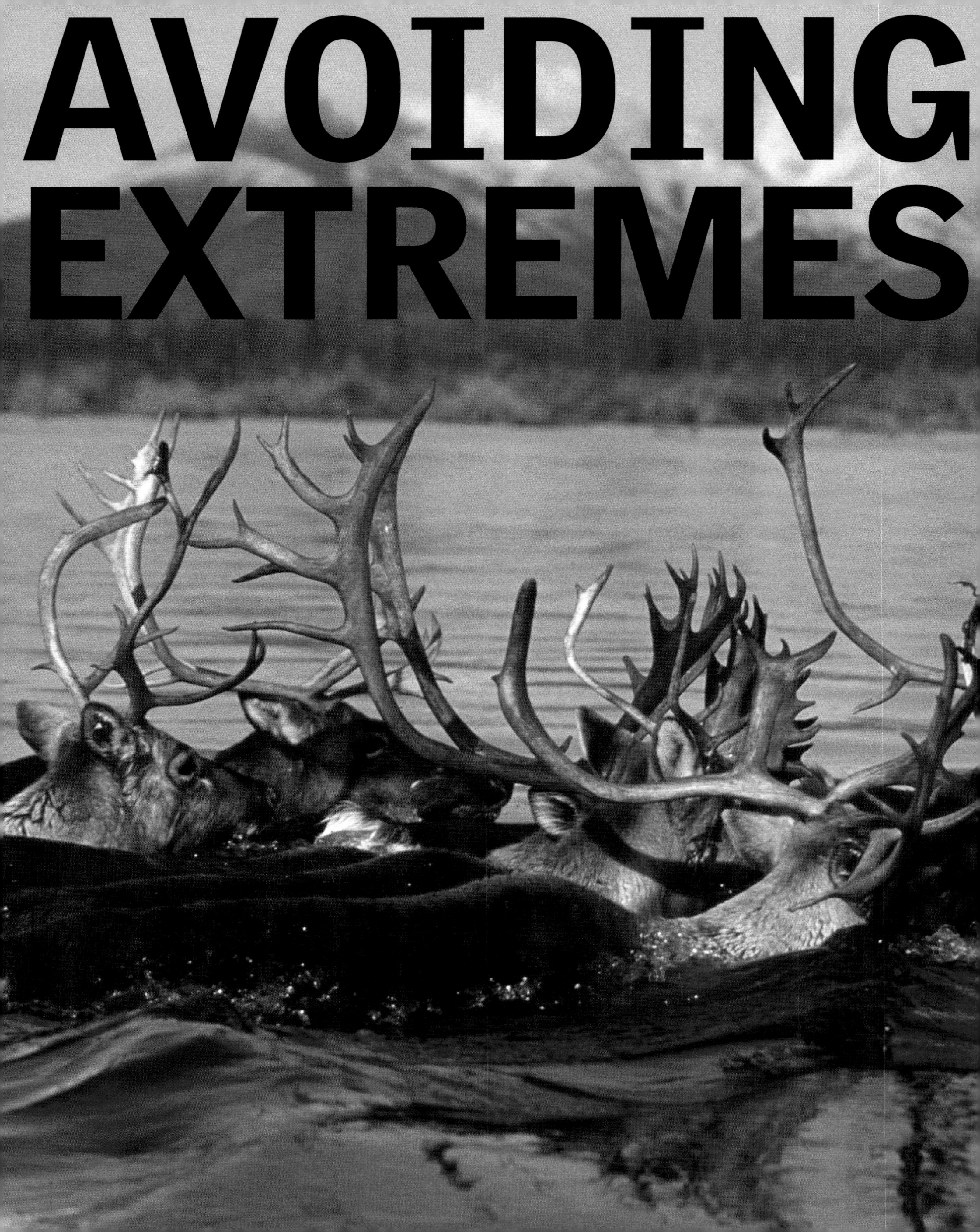

7

EXTREME WEATHER PUSHES ANIMALS TO THE LIMITS OF SURVIVAL. When temperatures veer towards extremes of either cold or heat, creatures have a number of options. Some migrate, like these caribou crossing the Kobuk River in Alaska. They move on to places where conditions are better, then return later in the year when things are more comfortable again. Others shut down for the duration, sleeping through times of adversity in a state of suspended animation. When cold triggers this state, it is known as hibernation; when too much heat is the problem, it is called aestivation (from the Latin *aestas*, 'summer'). Whichever option an animal takes – migration, hibernation or aestivation – it is a major disruption, for which the animal has to prepare itself, feeding while conditions are good to store away energy in the form of fat. If it is not ready, it will probably die.

TO PASTURES NEW

SOME CREATURES ARE ALWAYS ON THE MOVE, WHATEVER THE SEASON. They are the nomads of the animal world, regularly changing locations, moving on when food or water runs out in one place and seeking out new sources elsewhere. In the dry acacia scrub and grasslands of the Australian Outback, small chattering flocks of budgerigars are nomadic. Active in the early morning and late afternoon, the budgerigars spend as much time as they can close to waterholes, where they feed on the seeds of spinifex and other grasses. When they have devoured everything at one waterhole, they move elsewhere, leaving behind any young or sick birds that are unable to keep up with the flock. They seem able to sense from a distance where it has been raining and follow thunderstorms. If drought persists in the Outback, budgerigar flocks move into woodlands and coastal areas.

NOMADS ON THE MOVE A flock of wild budgerigars fills the sky in Sturt National Park, New South Wales. In the wild, these small parrots mostly have green abdomens and rumps, with yellow foreheads and faces when adult. Many are killed each year in bushfires, droughts and storms.

In favourable conditions, budgerigar flocks will join to form superflocks, some 20 000 strong – a pest for farmers, as the birds have a taste for ripening wheat. They also breed prolifically, with partnerships that last for life, nesting in holes in trees – usually river eucalypts – after periods of rain. Each pair raises four to six offspring, and if conditions remain good, they will raise another brood almost immediately. Predators include snakes, which sometimes enter the nests, but the budgerigars' biggest enemy is drought. During a drought in 1932, water and food were at such a premium that when budgerigars found an open waterhole, they descended on it in their thousands. Many were drowned by the sheer weight of their numbers, and millions died.

Armies on the move

African driver ants also have a nomadic lifestyle, in which a colony containing as many as 20 million ants regularly moves into a fresh area of rain forest and sets up camp. The colony establishes a bivouac constructed entirely – walls, corridors and chambers – from the ants themselves. From there, raiding parties spread out on a front about 15 m wide, with supply lines running back to base. The workers are all blind, so they track down prey by smell and vibration. If one ant senses something edible, it latches on with its large mandibles (mouthparts) and exudes an alarm pheromone that summons every ant nearby. The ants swarm all over their prey, slicing it into pieces that are easy to carry, taking back some 150 000 fragments from a single raid. When they have stripped that part of the forest bare, they move on. The entire driver ant army moves every 23 days or so.

NEW BIVOUAC When moving camp, a column of African driver ants passes at a rate of 250 000 ants per hour. The workers, carrying larvae and pupae, travel along a living avenue protected by soldiers on either side.

MIGRATION

IN THE NOT SO DISTANT PAST, PEOPLE WERE PUZZLED ABOUT WHY ANIMALS ARE HERE ONE MOMENT AND GONE THE NEXT. As late as the 18th century, it was widely thought in Europe that swallows buried themselves for winter in the mud at the bottoms of lakes. When scientists discovered that they fly to Africa and then return again in the spring, the fact of these extraordinary transglobal migrations seemed almost harder to believe than the myth.

Gradually, even more remarkable journeys came to light. Each autumn, Arctic terns fly from the Arctic and sub-Arctic to the Southern Ocean, then return again the following spring – a round trip of more than 38 000 km. White-rumped sandpipers spend part of the year north of the Arctic Circle, in Canada and Alaska, and the other part in southern South America. Sooty shearwaters fly a figure-of-eight course across the entire Pacific Ocean from New Zealand to Alaska and back again, travelling 900 km a day and diving to depths of up to 68 m to catch food. This journey of 62 800 km is the world's longest migration.

Why do the birds make these journeys? The answer is for food. They use the freedom of their wings to fly to places where

ARCTIC INFLUX Part of Alaska's Porcupine Herd of caribou migrates towards the state's northern coastal plain. Pregnant females and yearlings lead the way, followed by juveniles and males.

the pickings are best. Swallows feed on insects, and they find enough in Africa, but during the northern summer, the pickings are even better in northern temperate and tundra regions. In addition, the days are longer, which means more time to harvest the insect riches. It makes biological sense to breed and raise offspring in regions with the optimum food resources.

So why not stay all year? Habitats that are productive in summer may be far from fruitful in winter, and the closer to the poles the migrants fly, the worse the winter gets. The result is a mass movement of birds – geese, swans, ducks, shorebirds, seabirds and songbirds – all seeking places to spend the winter.

Great northern trek

Land animals migrate for similar reasons. In Siberia, Alaska and northern Canada, large herds of caribou (wild reindeer) spend the summer in the north of their range, where they drop their calves and eat well, then move south again for the winter. Scientists have given the herds names – the largest include the Western Arctic Herd in western Alaska, the George River Herd in northern Quebec and the Taimyr Peninsula Herd in northern Siberia. Each of these is estimated to be 500 000 strong.

CRAB CARPET Christmas Island's red land crabs are about 11 cm across. Their annual migration is synchronised across the entire island, linked to the phases of the Moon and the onset of the monsoon.

One closely studied group is Alaska's smaller Porcupine Herd of 123 000 animals. The herd migrates each spring from winter sites in forests south of the Brooks Range to summer calving and feeding grounds on the northern coastal plains and hills. It would be a journey of 640 km as the crow flies, but the caribou zigzag across the tundra, covering upwards of 4830 km each year. They travel in long lines, each caribou following the one in front, to the accompaniment of a constant clicking noise. Sounding rather like castanets, this is caused by tendons moving around bones in the caribou's feet. The hair of their long winter coat, which is hollow to trap air and keep the animals warm, is also handy when on migration as it helps to keep them afloat as they cross rivers.

Wolves are the main enemy of the caribou in their winter home. In summer, eagles take calves, while lynx and grizzly bears bring down adults. Wolverines kill the young, sick and elderly, and scavenge on leftover carcasses along with ravens. By far the biggest summer problem comes from micro-predators – blood-sucking mosquitoes and blackflies. Mosquitoes breed in tundra ponds in staggering numbers and can take so much blood from a caribou that it is left considerably weakened. To get away from the bugs, the caribou move to higher windy areas or places where patches of snow still cover the ground. The problem with this is that the caribou may not be able to feed properly – they may lose weight when they should be putting it on for the winter.

Christmas Island crabs

A shorter, but spectacular, land migration takes place on Christmas Island in the Indian Ocean, triggered by the arrival of the monsoon in October or November each year. The migrants are endemic red land crabs. When the monsoon arrives, they creep out of the forest, where they spend most of their lives, in order to breed by the sea. In five days, they travel about 8 km from the forest to the beach.

The red land crab population is estimated to be about 120 million. During the migration, there are so many of the creatures on the move – averaging about 65 million each year – that traffic comes to a halt and people board up their houses to prevent the crabs from getting in. The males go first to stake out the breeding beaches, then wait for the females – when all the crabs arrive, there could be as many as 100 per square metre. Mating occurs in shallow burrows excavated by the males. When the females are ready to spawn, they move to the water's edge and shake their eggs into the water.

Egg-laying complete, the adult crabs make the return trek to the forest. Their larvae develop in the sea for about a month, providing a feast for whale sharks and manta rays, which come to sieve them from the water. When the time is right, the surviving larvae emerge from the sea, colouring the rocks red. After five days, they moult into tiny air-breathing land crabs, just 5 mm across. They take about nine days to move into the forest, where they continue to moult and grow very slowly for the first three or four years of their lives. When mature, in their turn, they make the trek to the sea.

On the Caribbean island of Cuba, red, orange and yellow land crabs make a similar mass migration during March and April each year. Roads along the island's southern coast become jammed with the creatures and cars squash many of them, but the crabs get their own back as their tough exoskeletons puncture car tyres – hundreds each season. In 2001, the crabs' annual

SAND FIGHT Sand martins at nestholes in a sand wall near the Bolshoi Ugan River in Siberia: they return here each spring from overwintering sites in Africa.

NATURAL BIRD FOOD A female Eleonora's falcon mother brings a small songbird to feed her chicks. The prey was intercepted in Greece on its southerly autumn migration from Europe to Africa.

excursion had unexpected consequences during 40th-anniversary commemorations of the failed invasion at the Bay of Pigs, when a convoy of press cars accompanying visiting US dignitaries came to a halt, because crab debris had punctured the tyres of every car.

Finding their way

Long migratory journeys are rarely continuous. Birds that migrate prepare for their journey by putting on fat as fuel. Even so, their migrations are usually broken into short hops with refuelling stops. Also, if weather conditions are bad, especially if there are strong headwinds, the birds will put down and wait for better weather – there is evidence that they can detect small changes in air pressure that give an indication of weather conditions ahead.

Large birds, such as geese and swans, often travel by day, while most small bird migrants, such as songbirds, fly at night. Night fliers tend to be solitary, while daytime migrants travel in loose flocks, often in family groups. The night fliers take off at twilight, set their course with the aid of polarised light (vibrating light waves) from the setting Sun and navigate by the patterns of stars in the night sky. The day fliers use the Sun. Both types may take advantage of additional cues related to the Earth's magnetic field to establish where they are – a 'map' – and where they are heading – a 'compass'. When close to their destination, both night and day fliers seem to look out for landmarks to help them as they cover the last few kilometres. Astonishingly, arrivals and departures are often at the same time and date each year.

As well as adhering to timetables, the birds also travel along regular flyways – coastlines, mountain chains and narrow crossing points over the sea. It is possible that youngsters learn the routes, along with the locations of the stopover sites, from the older birds. All this makes their passage predictable, and predators take full advantage. On Mediterranean islands, Eleonora's

AMBUSH IN THE MASAI MARA
A leopard kills a wildebeest calf on migration. The leopard will haul the carcass to a tree to keep it safe from hyenas and lions.

falcons breed late in the season – in autumn, when the parent falcons can stake out crossing points along the southward route of small birds migrating to Africa. For the falcons and their chicks, this is a time of plenty; for the migrants, it is a hazard they must face every year. Flying at night is no safer – greater noctule bats intercept small songbirds, too.

River crossing

Ambushers also lurk in East Africa's Mara River. Nile crocodiles – 5 m long, disguised as logs but possessing jaws filled with fearsome rows of teeth – wait for the annual migration of wildebeest, zebras and Thomson's gazelles. The crocs seem to hear or feel the vibrations of millions of hooves, for by the time the first migrating animals arrive at the water's edge, the reptiles have already slipped into the water and are ready to grab and drown any they can clamp in their jaws. Waiting in the bush are prides of lions, preparing to ambush the migrating animals as they climb exhausted onto the opposite riverbank. The lions will feed well, too.

The migration itself is a considerable undertaking. Up to 1.4 million wildebeest and more than 200 000 zebra and gazelle travel more than 2900 km each year. There is no beginning and no end to the migration as the animals follow a clockwise path across the Serengeti Plains and through the Masai Mara. The precise direction depends on where the rain falls, promoting new growth. The wildebeest simply follow the rain and have an uncanny knack of heading the right way.

Another African migration, rivalling that of the wildebeest, is the journey made by a small antelope, the white-eared kob, in Sudan and Ethiopia. Up to a million kob travel 1500 km a year in search of water and food, along with 160 000 topi (also antelopes) and 250 000 Mongalla gazelles. As the animals move through grasslands and swamps, their columns can be 80 km long and 50 km across.

On the steppes of Central Asia and Europe, the saiga antelope migrates between grasslands in the northern steppe in summer and southern desert areas in winter, covering about 115 km a day during the journey. At one time, tens of thousands of saiga made the trek, but today, because of hunting, no more than 30 000 are thought to survive – the males' horns are prized in oriental medicine. One of the saiga's most noticeable characteristics is a large bulbous snout that hangs down over its mouth, which is thought to filter out dust as the animal migrates through dry grassland and semi-desert.

Tiny migrants

Not all transglobal migrants are birds or large mammals. Some smaller creatures travel astonishing distances, including monarch butterflies, which fly each autumn from Canada to California and Mexico to spend the winter there. Flapping their wings on average about five to twelve times per second and pursuing a dizzy, erratic course, the butterflies cover up to 425 km a day.

Unlike many birds, monarch butterflies cannot 'learn' the route because none of them have flown that way before – their life cycle lasts less than a year. Instead, the directions are 'hardwired' into them. They use the angle of polarised ultraviolet light from the Sun to find their way, then make in-flight adjustments employing a 'wiring' connection that links light-collecting sensors in the eyes with an internal clock. This enables the butterflies to compensate for the Sun's apparent movement across the sky – a time-compensated Sun compass. All this 'equipment' is contained in a creature that weighs just 0.5 grams.

In their wintering sites, the butterflies gather on the trunks of 'butterfly trees', mostly native sacred firs in Mexico and pines and introduced eucalypts in California. Here, they are protected from extremes of temperature, predators and bad weather until spring, when they head back north.

PAINTED LADY

ONE CHAMPION INSECT MIGRANT IS THE PAINTED LADY BUTTERFLY, WHICH TRAVELS UP TO 2000 KM FROM NORTH AFRICA TO EUROPE EACH YEAR. Setting out in January, as North Africa starts to warm up after the winter, flocks of the butterflies hitch a ride on winds blowing across the Mediterranean towards southern Europe. Breeding and dying as they go, they invade most parts of Europe, some individuals reaching Britain as early as February, although the bulk arrive in June. The last generation of the season returns south to Africa in August and September.

Different continents have different subspecies of painted lady. Although these vary, they are all large, with a wingspan up to 9 cm. Their coloration is orange with black spots and black and white corners to their wings. They lay their eggs on different plants, including thistles, hollyhocks and dwarf mallow, and the yellowish-green and black caterpillars feed on the same plants.

In North America, painted ladies spend the winter in subtropical north-western Mexico and southern California. When heavy rains come to the desert, they head north and north-east, sometimes in huge numbers. In the spring of 2005, billions of painted ladies fluttered into the Central Valley of California, one of the biggest painted lady migrations on record. Some individuals reached as far north as the Arctic Circle.

VITAL STATISTICS

ORDER: Lepidoptera
SPECIES: *Vanessa cardui*
HABITAT: Temperate zones, including mountains in the tropics
DISTRIBUTION: All continents except Antarctica
KEY FEATURES: Migrates in spring and autumn and is the most widespread species of butterfly.

TRAVELLERS AT SEA

MARINE CREATURES MAKE ASTONISHNG TRANSGLOBAL JOURNEYS. Every year, humpback whales travel between their winter homes in tropical and subtropical seas – such as the waters close to the West Indies, Costa Rica, Hawaii and Tonga – and their summer ranges in temperate and polar seas. The warmer seas are where they court, mate and calve; the cooler ones are rich in food. Whales in each hemisphere migrate mostly within that hemisphere – for example, humpbacks that overwinter around Tonga, in the Southern Hemisphere, head to the Antarctic in summer to feed, while those that mate around Hawaii in the Northern Hemisphere migrate to the waters off Alaska.

The population of about 3000–5000 humpbacks that overwinters off Hawaii includes females giving birth to calves, females ready to mate and bulls that fight for the females. The humpback bulls sing the longest songs of any animal – lasting up to two hours, the songs are believed to be a means of attracting mates, a way of communicating and a navigation aid. All this activity is done without feeding, so by

ANTARCTIC SOJOURN Emperor penguins travel up to 900 km from breeding sites on the Antarctic ice to feeding sites in the Southern Ocean. They walk part of the way over ice, swim the rest and dive to depths of 400 m when they get there.

TRANS-OCEAN JOURNEY

In 2005, marine biologists satellite-tagged a 4 m long female great white shark off South Africa and then tracked her as she travelled to waters off Western Australia – a distance of 11 000 km – in just three months. Nicknamed Nicole, the shark (right) swam almost in a straight line, indicating good navigational abilities. She spent most of the time near the surface, but dived occasionally to depths of 980 m. Within six months she was back in South African waters – the first shark to be tracked across an entire ocean and back. Other great whites tagged off California go to a mysterious area, dubbed the 'shark café' by researchers, midway between the North American mainland and Hawaii. What the sharks are doing there has yet to be discovered.

early spring the whales are more than ready to head north to seas filled with food. For the first third of their journey, they pursue a course that lies within one degree of magnetic North. It is thought that they use the Earth's magnetic field to navigate.

At their destination, the humpbacks feed on shrimp-like krill, herring and other small fish, before heading back south in the autumn for another four to six months of fasting. Every year, some whales try out new breeding sites in waters off Baja California or Japan, but they all return to the same feeding grounds off Alaska in summer.

Pacific exodus

Grey whales in the Pacific undertake an even longer migration. They spend their winters off Baja California and migrate north along North America's Pacific coast to the Bering Sea, where they feed on bottom-living crustaceans. Their journey of over 19 000 km is one of the longest migrations of any mammal.

While the grey whales are passing offshore, inshore waters along the Californian coast are the winter home of northern elephant seals, which haul out onto remote beaches, such as Ano Nuevo and Morro Bay, to drop their pups, mate and moult. Then, in spring, they head into the open ocean. Males make their way north-west to feeding grounds off Alaska, while females go into the middle of the Pacific, half way to Hawaii, feeding deep down in the ocean.

In the Southern Hemisphere, the world's largest seal, the southern elephant seal, migrates thousands of kilometres to and from feeding sites in the Southern Ocean, while another Antarctic animal, the emperor penguin, makes an extraordinary overland trek between the continent's ice edge and breeding sites far inland. This journey, which takes place during the Antarctic winter, can be up to 200 km long, sometimes in blizzard conditions, with the temperature dropping to –45°C. Once the penguins have mated, the male is left with an egg balanced on its feet during the worst of the cold weather.

LEFT BEHIND

The Sahara slowly became the hot, dry zone it is today, many of its animals dying out or moving elsewhere. But in oases fed by underground springs, a few of these creatures hung on and, thousands of years later, some still do, including Nile crocodiles.

CLIMATE CHANGE HAS PUSHED SOME SPECIES TO THE VERY LIMITS OF SURVIVAL IN REGIONS WHERE ONCE THEY WERE PLENTIFUL. As members of the species responded to the new conditions, many migrated to different homes better suited to them, but some – known as 'relict species' – got left behind. The pockets where they survive are called 'refugia'.

Until about 3400 BC, what is now the Sahara was green, fertile land, not desert. Prehistoric rock paintings show that Nile crocodiles lived across the region. Then came a change in the climate. The Sahara slowly became the hot, dry zone it is today, many of its animals dying out or moving elsewhere. But in oases fed by underground springs, a few of these creatures hung on and, thousands of years later, some still do, including Nile crocodiles. In the western Sahara, crocodiles live in Mauritania's Tagant Plateau, where scarcely any rain falls for long periods and wetlands, a normal habitat for crocodiles, dry up for months on end. In all, eight populations have been discovered across Mauritania, while reports from people living elsewhere along the Sahara's southern edge suggest that crocodiles survive in about 20 other places. Further relict populations are known to exist in the Guelta d'Archei and Ennedi Mountains in Chad; crocodiles also live on in caves on the island of Madagascar.

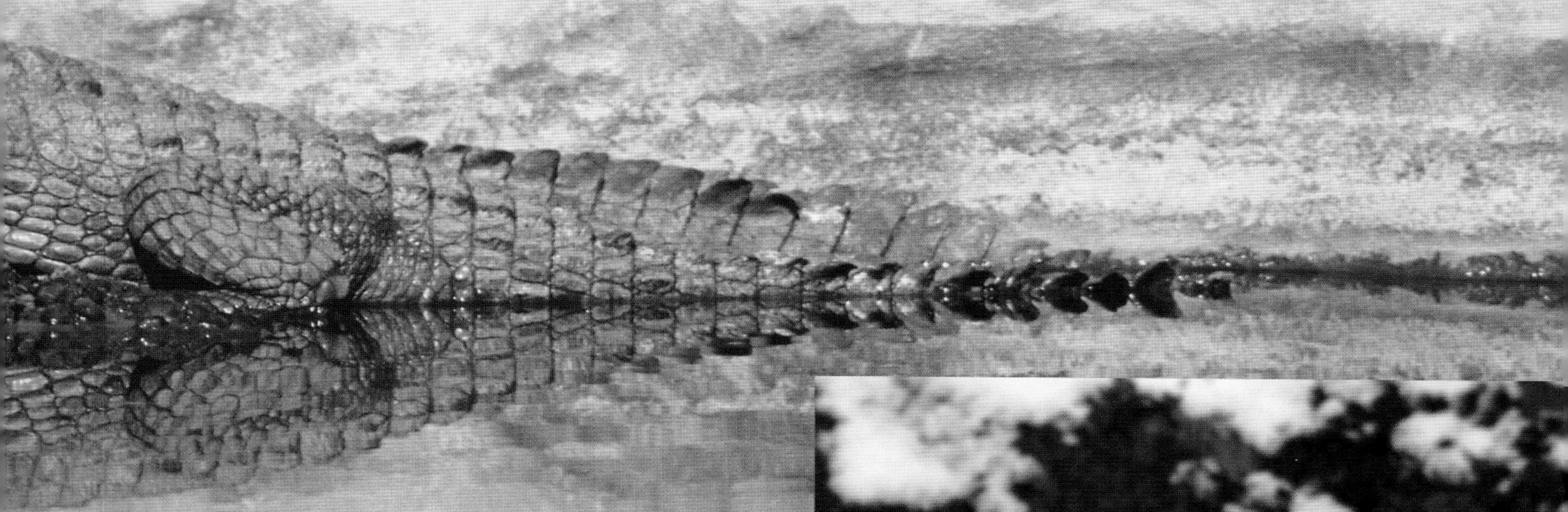

DESERT CROCS Nile crocodiles survive in isolated places in the southern fringe of the Sahara, a lingering reminder of greener conditions that once prevailed in the region.

The reptiles survive by hiding in caves and burrows and under rocks. During dry periods, they go into a kind of torpor, in which they do not eat and keep movement to a minimum, although they may come out at night. They are considerably smaller than their relatives in East and southern Africa – little more than 1.5–2 m long, compared to a more usual 5 m.

Arctic Scotland

In the Scottish Highlands, several animal species are relicts from a time when an ice sheet covered two-thirds of the British Isles and much of Northern Europe. When the ice retreated at the end of the last ice age, about 10 000 years ago, creatures such as ptarmigan, Arctic hares and snow buntings – all species normally found much farther north – stayed behind in the Cairngorms, where arctic conditions persist through much of the winter.

Ptarmigan, in particular, are perfectly adapted to the cold. Feathers cover their entire bodies, including their legs and feet, and they have a kind of internal central heating system powered by friendly bacteria in the gut. With their white winter plumage, the birds almost disappear when sitting in a snow hollow during a blizzard. Then, in summer, they switch to mottled brown, which camouflages them amid the heather. Arctic hares undergo a similar transformation, alternating between a white winter coat and a brown summer one, but this system sometimes goes wrong in spring. The hares may be caught out wearing their winter coat after the snow has melted, making them very obvious targets for the region's supreme predator – the golden eagle.

Elsewhere in Europe, relict populations of another ice age survivor, the Arctic char (a relative of trout and salmon), are found in several lakes, including those of the English Lake District. During the last ice age, glaciers gouged out U-shaped valleys in these regions, and when the glaciers melted, they left behind strings of ribbon-like lakes with populations of the fish trapped in them. Today, the Arctic char survives in Britain as one of its rarest fish.

SNOW CHICKEN A hen ptarmigan in white winter plumage is well insulated against the icy conditions that prevail in Scotland's Cairngorm Mountains in winter.

ICE RELICT Mostly found in Arctic and sub-Arctic lakes, the Arctic char also survives in Alpine lakes, such as the Grundlsee in Austria (here), as a relict from the last ice age.

SHUTTING DOWN

MIGRATION IS ONE WAY TO AVOID THE WORST OF A REGION'S WEATHER AND THE LACK OF FOOD THAT GENERALLY RESULTS. Another is to sleep through those times when active survival is simply not possible. When the temperature plummets, some animals shut down their entire body and go into a state of hibernation. The animal's body temperature drops – ground squirrels, for example, can reduce their body temperature to –2°C, matching the ambient air temperature – while the rate of breathing slows and the metabolic rate lowers. The hibernating animal relies on stores of body fat to keep it going at this lower metabolic rate. The state of dormancy can last for several weeks or even months. In some animals, the sleep of hibernation is continuous through the winter; in others, it is broken by brief spells of activity.

The hibernating animal's body temperature drops – ground squirrels can reduce their body temperature to –2°C, matching the air temperature – while the rate of breathing slows and the metabolic rate lowers.

Not surprisingly, most animals that hibernate live in colder regions. Bats, hedgehogs, dormice, western diamondback rattlesnakes, certain lemurs, ground

DEEP SLEEP A Richardson's ground squirrel in southern Alberta, Canada, is a true hibernator. It rarely stirs its body during the winter.

squirrels and other rodents and insectivores all hibernate; no primates and few tropical mammals are known to do so. One tropical exception is Madagascar's fat-tailed dwarf lemur, which hibernates in treetrunks for more than half the year, even though winter temperatures in Madagascar can be as high as 30°C. In the case of the dwarf lemur, it is believed to be hibernating to avoid the drier months of the year, surviving on fat stored in its tail.

One animal that is often said to hibernate is the brown bear – including its subspecies, North America's grizzly bear – but the bear's inactivity during winter is not true hibernation. Inside its den for the winter, the brown bear maintains a body temperature of 31°C, only a few degrees down from its active temperature of 37°C, compared, for example, to the –2°C body temperature of a hibernating ground squirrel. This allows the animal to galvanise itself quickly into action if danger threatens. Even so, the brown bear shares a physiological state with true hibernators, the result of a substance called the 'hibernation induction trigger' (HIT), which is present in the blood of all hibernating creatures. As its name suggests, HIT induces animals to hibernate – if taken from a hibernating animal and injected into a non-hibernating one, it causes the latter to hibernate. Scientists believe that HIT might be useful for organ transplants in humans, as it could increase the length of time an organ survives outside the body.

Temporary shutdown

Another way in which animals slow down in response to colder weather is called diapause. This occurs when an animal stops development during the winter and then continues again in the spring. Some insects do this, as do a few mammals. The female red deer, for instance, delays the attachment of the embryo to the uterus wall. This ensures that the embryo develops for a birth in spring, when conditions are best for it to develop and grow.

Another process similar to hibernation is brumation, seen in some reptiles. In response to shortening days, the reptiles undergo a state of semi-dormancy, in which they seem extremely lethargic and sleep for long periods of time. Small birds, such as hummingbirds, and some species of bat go into a state of torpor – a reduction in body temperature and metabolic rate that lasts for short periods. For some of these creatures, their level of activity is normal during the day, but then drops in response to cold temperatures at night.

INTERRUPTED SLEEP A European brown bear emerges in a somewhat dazed state from its winter den. The bear does not undergo true hibernation, but sleeps on and off through the worst days.

WINTER FOR INVERTEBRATES

IN TEMPERATE LATITUDES, INSECTS GENERALLY OPT OUT OF WINTER. Some, such as the monarch and painted lady butterflies (see pages 142 and 143), head for warmer climes, but the majority of insects stay put, searching out stable microhabitats where they can spend the winter – under logs, in leaf litter, inside rotting logs, in bark cracks and in plant galls. A few find refuge in caves and tunnels. Most insects are fine in these places so long as temperatures do not fluctuate wildly between thaws and freezing. A number have antifreeze compounds (see page 42), which keep their bodies from freezing solid – if they freeze, they are dead.

Sheltered places

Among non-migratory butterflies and moths, most live through the winter as eggs, larvae or pupae, which lie hidden in leaf litter or similarly protected places and continue their development in spring. Beetles generally dig deep underground. Ladybirds cluster together and shut down in dead wood, hollow plant stems or other sheltered places, including attics and barns. Houseflies and bluebottles hibernate in the cellars and attics of buildings. Cockroaches and firebrats also enjoy the protection of our homes, while lice and fleas have the warmth of their warm-blooded hosts.

In wasp colonies, the workers die in autumn and only the queen survives until spring. It is the same for bumblebee queens, which burrow down in the earth to levels beyond the reach of frost. In a colony of honeybees, many individuals live on, as well as the queen, but they are relatively inactive. They generate warmth by vibrating their muscles, drawing on their stores of honey as fuel, then use their wings to waft the heat around the colony.

The aquatic nymphs of dragonflies, mayflies and stoneflies survive very well under ice in ponds and streams. At a time when most other insects have shut down, the nymphs continue their development, so they emerge as adults before other insects in spring. In Romania's Kedrovaya Pad Preserve, chironomid mosquitoes get a head start. In January, when the air temperature may be as low as –25°C, the mosquitoes emerge from patches of the Kedrovaya River where the ice has thawed in the winter Sun. They mate, lay eggs and then die.

Among other invertebrates, the adults in some spider species die in winter, leaving their eggs protected in silken cocoons tucked under logs; in other species, the adults hibernate inside cocoons. Land snails find sheltered places, where they lock themselves away inside their shells, with an operculum (cover) and mucous plug to isolate them from the rigours outside.

WINTER HUDDLE Ladybirds go for company in winter. Here, a cluster of seven-spot ladybirds hibernates on a thorn bush. Sometimes, hundreds of individuals come together like this.

COMMON POORWILL

ONE BIRD KNOWN TO USE DEEP TORPOR

TO GET THROUGH THE WINTER IS THE COMMON POORWILL. A nocturnal bird related to nightjars, the poorwill lives in dry, open areas in western North America, from British Columbia as far south as northern Mexico. Many individuals migrate in winter, but those in the southern part of the poorwill's range become inactive instead. Sheltering among rocks, they slow their metabolic rate and allow their body temperature to drop until they enter a hibernation-like state of torpor, which enables them to survive cold spells when their insect prey is scarce. Poorwills can remain in torpor for weeks or even months.

The behaviour was first described scientifically in 1946, when ornithologist Edmund Jaeger came across a hibernating poorwill in the Chuckwalla Mountains of California. In fact, it had been observed before, in what is now North Dakota in 1804, when the explorer Meriwether Lewis wrote about it in his diary during his expedition with William Clark across North America. Native Americans of the Hopi tribe were well aware of the bird and its winter behaviour, and called it the *holchko*, 'sleeping one'. Its name in English is onomatopoeic for the call it makes – a loud 'poor-will'.

VITAL STATISTICS

CLASS: Aves
ORDER: Caprimulgiformes
SPECIES: *Phalaenoptilus nuttallii*
HABITAT: Open grassland and scrub
DISTRIBUTION: Western part of North America
KEY FEATURES: Active at night; it goes into hibernation-like torpor in winter.

MOUNTAIN RETREAT Every summer, vast numbers of Bogong moths (see page 104) escape the heat in southern Australia by fluttering high into the mountain ranges that straddle the border of New South Wales and Victoria. Here, they aestivate in rock crevices and caves.

SUMMER SLEEPERS

WHILE HIBERNATION ALLOWS ANIMALS TO SURVIVE THE COLD, AESTIVATION IS A WAY OF COPING WITH THE HEAT. It is a state of dormancy, similar to hibernation, but occurring in summer when temperatures soar and water is scarce. In North America, the California red-legged frog lives for much of the year in lush, shrubby vegetation alongside deep, still or slow-running water. In mid-summer, as temperatures reach 30°C or more, it retreats into rodent burrows or under damp leaf litter, where it hides from the Sun and temporarily shuts down its body.

In Australia, the water-holding frog does something similar. Living in grasslands, depressions in the ground and ditches, it owes its common name to its ability to store water in its bladder and in pockets under the skin. At the hottest times of the year, when the frog's habitat dries up for weeks or even months on end, it goes underground, digging down into the damp earth to create a burrow. It secretes a mucous lining to the underground chamber and wraps a cocoon around itself consisting of layers of mucous and dried skin. The chamber and jacket protect the frog from the heat and prevent water from evaporating. After rain falls and the surrounding area floods, it emerges and restocks its in-built reservoirs by absorbing water through its skin.

For Australia's Aboriginal people, the water-holding frog is familiar from a character called Tiddalik, who features in the Dreamtime stories that tell of the island continent's history and natural history. In summer, when water is scarce, people sometimes dig up the frogs and press them gently. This causes them to release some of their water, which is surprisingly fresh.

Slow burrowers

Also in Australia, tropical freshwater turtles aestivate when their ponds dry up. One species shows unusual nesting behaviour, which actually takes advantage of the drought. Baby turtles have to hatch out on land, and most turtles deposit their eggs on sandy beaches, but the female Siebenrock's side-necked turtle deposits hers in an underwater nest in a pond. The eggs lie dormant until the pond dries up, at which point the eggs develop and the youngsters can hatch out normally.

Another aestivator is the desert tortoise of North America's Mojave and Sonoran deserts. The creature burrows underground to escape temperatures that can climb to 60°C. In fact, the tortoise spends about 95 per cent of its life underground and some of this

LIVING RESERVOIR In hot drought conditions, Australia's water-holding frog buries itself in the ground with a store of water in its body. It emerges when the rains return.

time can be considered hibernation, since it also becomes dormant when winter temperatures plunge to zero. For the 5 per cent of its existence that it is active above ground, the desert tortoise feeds mainly on grasses, obtaining most of its annual supply of water from food consumed in spring. It has a large urinary bladder that stores 40 per cent of its body-weight as water and natural waste. Any urine that is voided appears as a white paste – another water-conservation measure. Thus equipped, desert tortoises can survive for a year or more without access to water.

Hibernators also aestivate

The same snails that hibernate in winter (see page 150) may also aestivate in hot summers. They find suitable hiding places and then seal off the entrance to their shells with an operculum to conserve water. In North America, apple snails do this when the wetland areas they live in dry out, remaining inactive until rain falls and water returns. In Florida, where apple snails are common, the adults

VENTURING OUT A desert tortoise emerges from its burrow in California's Mojave Desert. The ability to retreat underground allows the tortoise to survive where temperatures range from freezing to 60°C.

can survive for three to four months in this way. Youngsters are not so resilient. Newly hatched snails would dry out quickly, so the adult snails lay their eggs early enough in the season to enable their youngsters to develop sufficiently before the drought.

Earthworms also shut down when the surface soil dries out. They burrow down to where the soil is still moist and create a mucous-lined chamber in which they curl up in a knot, reduce their oxygen intake, turn pink and remain dormant for weeks. They do the same thing when it gets cold, so earthworms both aestivate and hibernate, always in a knot. Palaeontologists (fossil hunters) have found fossil earthworm chambers in rocks dating back to about 125 000 years ago.

PLANTS ON THE EDGE

PLANTS CANNOT ESCAPE EXTREMES OF WEATHER IN THE WAY THAT ANIMALS DO, but they are good at preparing themselves for tough times ahead. In temperate regions, they do this by always being one step ahead of the seasons, a strategy that is most strikingly visible in autumn, when the leaves of deciduous trees change colour. The process takes a couple of weeks to get going, triggered by shortening days, temperature change and late summer drying. The trees begin to withdraw water from their leaves, and these, in turn, are sealed off from the rest of the plant by a corky membrane.

Pigment change

At the same time, chemical changes are taking place in the photosynthetic pigments in the leaves' cells. The green leaves of summer contain mostly chlorophyll, which plants use, together with sunlight and carbon dioxide, to form sugars. As the season changes and less light is available, plants produce less chlorophyll but more xanthocyanins – red pigments, which act like a sunscreen, protecting the other pigments as the plants reabsorb them. Yellow carotenoids, a secondary photosynthetic pigment, break down

TOUGH WOOD Caribou graze under a Siberian larch, an example of a deciduous (as opposed to evergreen) conifer, whose needle-like leaves turn brown and fall from the tree in autumn. Many traditional Russian houses and churches were built from the wood of the Siberian larch, because of its resistance to rot.

PROTECTIVE PLANT A Californian coastal agave has its own way of dealing with changing conditions. During a prolonged drought, its succulent leaves close together to protect the plant's young leaves (left). In wet years, the plant opens up to its more usual rosette shape (right).

more slowly than chlorophyll, so their colour begins to show through, turning leaves orange. As the red pigments are lost, the leaves turn yellow, and when much of the yellow pigment has been reabsorbed, the leaves turn brown, the colour of lignin – one of the chief constituents of wood.

Evergreen conifers, including the pines and cypresses, do none of this. They have needle-like leaves, such as those of pines, or scale-like ones, like cypresses. These lose very little water, so the tree can afford to keep them throughout both summer and winter – conifers can keep the same leaves for up to 40 years, although it is rare that they do so. The sap in conifers also contains antifreeze, one of the adaptations that have allowed pines to become the most widespread group of trees on Earth.

ARCTIC BEAUTY The evergreen mountain avens is one of a number of plants that survive plunging Arctic temperatures and violent winds by growing in clumps close to the ground.

INDEX

T

UV

W

YZ

PICTURE CREDITS

Abbreviations: T = top; B = bottom; L = left; R = right

Front cover: ardea.com/M.Watson
Back cover: FLPA/Patricio Robles Gil/Sierra Madre/Minden Pictures.

1 naturepl.com/Grant McDowell. **2–7** photolibrary.com/Zhinong Xi. **3** Hedgehog House/Dick & Pip Smith, ML; Getty Images/Daisy Gilardini, MR; FLPA/Michael Gore, M; Still Pictures/Biosphoto/Antoine Dervaux, BL; Guillaume Dargaud, BR. **3–4** naturepl.com/Vincent Munier, TR. **4** ardea.com/François Gohier, TR; National Geographic Image Collection/Peter Carsten, TM; Corbis/Martin Harvey, M; Image Quest Marine/Peter Batson, MB; Ian MacDonald, BR. **5** FLPA/Imagebroker/Jochen Tack, TL; DRK PHOTO/Donald M. Jones, TR; Photolibrary Group/Robert Harding Travel/R.Mcleod, ML; Still Pictures/Biosphoto/Xavier Eichaker, MR; Image Quest Marine/Peter Batson, BL. **5–6** naturepl.com/Owen Newman. **6** Science Photo Library/Simon Fraser, TL; Provided by Michael J. Daly, Uniformed Services University of the Health Sciences, Betheseda. Maryland, TR; Photolibrary Group/SGM SGM, ML; Corbis/Ralph White, MR; Photolibrary Group/Phototake Science/Dennis Kunkel. **8–9** Still Pictures/Biosphoto/Klein J.-L. & Hubert M.-L. **10–11** left to right: Getty Images/Theo Allofs, 1; ardea.com/Andrey Zvoznikov, 2; FLPA/Elliott Neep, 3; National Geographic Image Collection/Bill Curtsinger, 4; Still Pictures/A. Hartl, 5; Still Pictures/McPhoto, 6; Photoshot/Daniel Heuclin, 7. **12–13** left to right: Photolibrary Group/Animals Animals/Earth Scenes/David Fritts, 1; FLPA/Frans Lanting, 2, 3; ardea.com/Jean Paul Ferrero, 4; Getty Images/National Geographic/Timothy Laman, 5; Photolibray Group/David B. Fleetham, 6; Still Pictures/Wildlife/H. Schweiger (background). **14–15** DRK Photo/Thomas Dressler. **16** FLPA/B. Borrell Casals, BL. **16–17** naturepl.com/Tom Vezo. **17** imagequestmarine.com/Peter Batson, TR. **18–19** naturepl.com/Jason Venus. **19** ardea.com/Steve Downer, TL. **20** DRK PHOTO/Pete Oxford. **21** Auscape/Roger Brown, TR; Photoshot/Anthony Bannister, B. **22** DRK PHOTO/Martin Harvey. **23** Still Pictures/H. Schmidbauer, TL; Photoshot/Daniel Heuclin, BR. **24–25** Olivier Grunewald. **26** Olivier Grunewald. **27** naturepl.com/Gertrud & Helmut Denzau. **28** naturepl.com/Cindy Buxton. **28–29** ardea.com/Jean Paul Ferrero. **29** Photoshot/NHPA/J. & A. Scott, TR. **30** Photoshot/NHPA/Daniel Heuclin. **31** naturepl.com/Premaphotos/Ken Preston-Mafham, TL. **30–31** FLPA/Minden Pictures/Patricio Robles Gil/Sierra Madre (background). **32** Photolibrary Group/OSF. **32–33** FLPA/Malcolm Schuyl. **34–35** Getty Images/Theo Allofs. **35** ardea.com/Bob Gibbons, BR. **36–37** FLPA/Minden Pictures/Thomas Mangelsen. **38–39** Hedgehog House/Colin Monteath. **39** ardea.com/Andrey Zvoznikov, BR. **40** Still Pictures/Biosphoto/BIOS-Auteurs/Stoeckle Tanguy. **41** Getty Images/Norbert Wu. **42** DRK PHOTO/Tom Till. **43** Photoshot/NHPA/T. Kitchen & V. Hurst. **44** Getty Images/Minden Pictures/Norbert Wu. **45** National Geographic Image Collection/Paul Nicklen. **46** ardea.com/Andrey Zvoznikov. **47** DRK PHOTO/Bob Gurr, TL. arcticphoto.co.uk/Bryan & Cherry Alexander Photography, B. **48** FLPA/Minden Pictures/Thomas Mangelsen, T; DRK PHOTO/Wayne Lynch, B. **49** naturepl.com/Mark Taylor. **50–51** Corbis/DLILLC. **52** FLPA/Minden Pictures/Tui De Roy. **53** Auscape/Dorothy Keeler. **54–55** FLPA/Elliott Neep. **56** naturepl.com/Pete Oxford, BL. **57** FLPA/Sunset. **58** naturepl.com/Sue Daly. **59** Photoshot/NHPA/Adrian Hepworth. **60** Origin Natural History Media/Dave Hansford. **61** Natural Visions/Heather Angel. **62** ardea.com/Pat Morris. **63** Still Pictures/WaterFrame/Wolfgang Poelzer. **64** Photoshot/NHPA/J. & A. Scott. **64–65** naturepl.com/Mark Payne-Gill. **66** Getty Images/National Geographic Image/Nicole Duplaix. **67** Photoshot/NHPA/Daniel Heuclin. **68–69** Still Pictures/Wildlife/J. Freund. **69** Photolibrary Group/David B. Fleetham. **70** Corbis/Martin Harvey, ML. **70–71** FLPA/Elliott Neep. **71** Alamy/Stone Nature Photography, TR. **72–73** Science Photo Library/David Aubrey. **74–75** FLPA/Frans Lanting. **76** Photolibrary Group/Oxford Scientific. **77** Science Photo Library/Merlin Tuttle. **78–79** naturepl.com/Neil Bromhall. **80** Corbis/Theo Allofs. **81** FLPA/Minden Pictures/Konrad Wothe, TL; ardea.com/Jean Paul Ferrero, R. **82** Getty Images/National Geographic/Stephen Alvarez, BR. **82–83** National Geographic Image Collection/Stephen Alvarez. **83** Photolibrary Group/Tobias Bernhard, TR; Still Pictures/Matt Meadows, B. **84–85** National Geographic Image Collection/Burt Curtsinger. **85** Still Pictures/Darlyne A. Murawski, TR. **86** FLPA/Reinhard Dirscherl. **86–87** naturepl.com/Nature Production. **88** imagequestmarine.com/Jim Greenfield. **88–89** National Geographic Image Collection/Tim Laman. **90–91** FLPA/John Holmes. **92–93** Still Pictures/A. Hartl. **93** Photolibrary Group/TC Nature, BR. **94–95** top to bottom, left to right: Photolibrary Group/OSF/John Downer, 1; naturepl.com/Barrie Britton, 2; Getty Images/Minden Pictures/Tui De Roy, 3; Jim Sanderson, 4; Sue Bishop, 5; ardea.com/Joanna Van Gruisen, 6; FLPA/Yuri Artukhin, 7. **96–97** Photolibrary Group/Animals Animals/Earth Scenes/David Fritts. **98** Photolibrary Group/Rachel Bomford/Tony Bomford. **99** Photolibrary Group/Juniors Bildarchiv. **100** Auscape/Tui De Roy. **101** FLPA/Sunset, T; Photoshot/NHPA/Eric Soder, BR. **102–103** Photolibrary Group/Index Stock Imagery/Lynn Stone. **104** Corbis/zefa/Christof Wermter. **105** Still Pictures/Wildlife/S. Muller. **106** Photolibrary Group/Colin Monteath. **107** Photolibrary Group/OSF/William Gray. **108** Auscape/Amy Gulick. **109** Still Pictures/Biosphoto/Georges Lopez. **110–111** Photolibrary Group/Panorama Media (Beijing) Ltd/Zhinong Xi. **112–113** FLPA/Bill Baston. **114–115** naturepl.com/John Waters. **115** FLPA/Nigel Cattlin, BR. **116** FLPA/Foto Natura/Rene Krekels. **116–117** FLPA/Frans Lanting. **118** Corbis/Momatiuk – Eastcott. **119** Photoshot/NHPA/Stephen Dalton, T; Photolibrary Group/Animals Animals/Earth Scenes/Raymond Mendez, B. **120** FLPA/Frans Lanting, BR. **120–121** Photoshot/NHPA/Cede Prudente. **121** FLPA/Minden Pictures/Tui De Roy, TR. **122** naturepl.com/Tom Vezo. **123** Getty Images/National Geographic/Timothy Laman. **124** Still Pictures/Wildlife/C. Gomersall, TL; naturepl.com/Nature Production, BR. **124–125** Still Pictures/McPhoto. **126** naturepl.com/Markus Varesvuo. **127** naturepl.com/Dietmar Nill. **128** naturepl.com/John Waters. **128–129** Still Pictures/Wildlife/H. Schweiger. **130–131** naturepl.com/Rolf Nussbaumer. **132** Getty Images/National Geographic/Bill Curtsinger. **133** Photoshot/NHPA/Kevin Schafer. **134–135** FLPA/Minden Pictures/Michio Hoshino. **136–137** naturepl.com/Owen Newman. **137** FLPA/Peter Davey, B. **138–139** FLPA/Minden Pictures/Michio Hoshino. **139** ardea.com/Jean Paul Ferrero, TR. **140** ardea.com/Andrey Zvoznikov. **141** FLPA/Minden Pictures/Konrad Wothe. **142** FLPA/Mark Newman. **143** naturepl.com/Premaphotos/Ken Preston-Mafham. **144–145** naturepl.com.Doug Allan. **145** Newspix Ltd/News Ltd/3rd Party Managed Reproduction & Supply Rights, TR. **146–147** Science Photo Library/George Steinmetz. **147** ardea.com/George Reszeter, MR; FLPA/R. Dirschert, BL. **148–149** Photoshot/NHPA/Daniel Heuclin. **149** DRK PHOTO/Wayne Lynch, TL. **150** naturepl.com/Jane Burton. **151** Still Pictures/Tom Vezo. **152** Photoshot/ANT Photo/Rob Blakers, TL; Auscape/Kathie Atkinson, BR. **153** FLPA/Minden Pictures/Larry Minden. **154–155** arcticphoto.co.uk/Bryan & Cherry Alexander Photography. **155** DRK Photo/David Cavagnaro, T; FLPA/Winfried Wisneiwski, B.

NATURE'S MIGHTY POWERS: LIFE AT THE LIMITS was published by The Reader's Digest Association Ltd, London. It was created and produced for Reader's Digest by Toucan Books Ltd, London.

The Reader's Digest Association Ltd,
11 Westferry Circus,
Canary Wharf,
London E14 4HE
www.readersdigest.co.uk

Written by
Michael Bright

FOR TOUCAN BOOKS
Editors Jane Chapman, Andrew Kerr-Jarrett, Chris Marshall
Designers Bradbury & Williams
Picture researchers Wendy Palmer, Sharon Southren, Mia Stewart-Wilson, Christine Vincent
Proofreader Marion Dent
Indexer Michael Dent

FOR READER'S DIGEST
Project editor Christine Noble
Art editor Julie Bennett
Pre-press account manager Dean Russell
Product production manager Claudette Bramble
Production controller Katherine Bunn

READER'S DIGEST, GENERAL BOOKS
Editorial director Julian Browne
Art director Anne-Marie Bulat

Colour origination Colour Systems Ltd, London
Printed and bound in China

We are committed to both the quality of our products and the service we provide to our customers. We value your comments, so please feel free to contact us on 08705 113366 or via our website at **www.readersdigest.co.uk**

If you have any comments or suggestions about the content of our books, you can email us at **gbeditorial@readersdigest.co.uk**

CONCEPT CODE: UK0138/G/S
BOOK CODE: 636-011 UP0000-1
ISBN: 978-0-276-44328-2
ORACLE CODE: 356500009H.00.24